WHAT

PRACTICAL ADVICE

MATTHEW L. MARTIN

WHAT NEXT?

PRACTICAL ADVICE FOR NEW CONVERTS

BY

MATTHEW
L. MARTIN

ISBN: 9798447922764

This book is copyright © 2022

www.booksbymatthew.com

TABLE OF CONTENTS

INTRODUCTION

For me, the water was cold, even though it was summertime. I was not prepared for the rush of chilly water enveloping my body. I wasn't baptized inside a church building. The vista of a long and winding creek (technically a bayou), with grass and trees growing wildly on either side, was not just a painting on the wall behind the baptistry; it was reality.

I was baptized at a church camp in Scottsville, Arkansas. As a person who never took swimming lessons, the prospect of wading waist-deep into running water was hardly a delightful one. And then there were the cows: Livestock regularly cooled themselves in that water. They probably relieved themselves in it too.

And in I went.

WHAT NEXT?

I distinctly remember the muffled *glub-glub* sound filling my ears as I plunged into the water. It was dark, early in the morning before sunrise on Friday the 23rd of June. I was fifteen, about to turn sixteen. I was shy and awkward. I had never taken an interest in public speaking, or really in anything that would put me in the center of attention. And yet there I was—with a dozen people watching, and many dozens more soon to pat me on the back when the sun rose—making a confession that I believed Jesus was the Christ and that I was ready to obey His command for all believers to be baptized to be saved (Mark 16:16).

My brother-in-law Chris lifted me out of the water barely two seconds after he lowered me in. The "oowah" sound of my ears breaking through the surface of the chilly creek was accompanied by a series of other noises I can only barely recall now twenty-two years later. I remember hearing a few people saying "amen." My friend Clay was one of them. I remember Chris saying "that's it, you're done." to me as he slapped my back. And I remember responding "I'm never doing that again."

At the time, I was thinking only of how nervous I was to be waist-deep in the creek. Half my attention was on keeping my footing. In the back of my mind, I wondered what would happen if I slipped and was carried away (the kind of extreme "what if" scenarios I like to think many teenagers imagine from time to time). Looking back, the first words I uttered after being immersed were hardly the most inspirational or befitting. I hadn't yet come to terms with what I had done or what lay in store for me.

I certainly understood what I did. I could recite the relevant scriptures and make the correct arguments for what I had done, but I was still only fifteen. What fifteen-year-old fully understands the consequences of his actions? What teenager is able to fathom the butterfly effect that can occur when a person makes a decision that others around him will either support or reject?

It's a tremendous thing to obey the Gospel. Without question becoming a Christian is the most important decision a person will ever make. Nothing compares to it because it concerns the everlasting life of the soul. And yet, at the moment I put on Christ, my first thought was only for how I was standing in a bayou and didn't know how to swim.

It wasn't until after a few hours of sleep that I finally began to contemplate the future. I awoke Friday morning, and how I felt on my first

WHAT NEXT?

full day as a child of God inspired something I have said many times in the years since.

I felt normal.

I didn't have any special tingling sensation. I didn't have warm bubbles in my stomach or an indescribable sense of enlightenment in my mind. I was the same person I was the day before. The only difference was what Christ had done for me. My salvation did not come with a physical transformation. Other than getting wet, I was, on the outside, the same person that went into the water as I was when I came out of the water.

What happened after that is my own story and it is unique to me. Everyone's personal experiences are individual but, as baptized believers, we all share one thing in common: We all belong to the body of Jesus. We've all been added by the Lord to His spiritual Kingdom.

And while the particulars of our lives are all different, it's safe to say that all of us, upon being baptized into Christ, have asked—in one way or another—the question on the cover of this book: What next?

I know what my brother-in-law meant when, upon baptizing me, he said "you're done." He was thinking of my nervousness being in the water. He wasn't talking about my life. He would tell you, as I will, that becoming a Christian is not the end.

It can feel like the end: Maybe you listened to the preacher as he finished his sermon and offered the invitation. Maybe you concluded a Bible study with a loved one and there were no more questions to answer. Maybe you were sitting on your bed, crying after stumbling into some horrible situation without any way of escape; at the end of your rope, you realized you needed to change the direction of your life. All of those scenarios involve an ending, a feeling of completion or finality.

When you obey the Gospel after the invitation is extended, it can feel like you put a neat and tidy bow on the day's events. When you obey the Gospel after finishing a Bible study, it can feel like you're doing the last thing that's involved in the sit-down course. No matter how you slice it, being baptized feels like the end.

It is not.

You're not done when you obey the Gospel; you're just getting started. To be sure, a lot of things **are** ended, but the process that began with your hearing the Gospel, which led to your belief, the repentance of your sins, and your readiness to confess your faith in Christ, does not draw to a close when you obey the Lord's command to be immersed. Instead, the blood that covers your sins upon your salvation continually covers your sins

WHAT NEXT?

from that point until the end, for as long as you walk in His light (1 John 1:10).

You are only just beginning to live a new kind of life. You are only just setting out to take steps in the light of Christ. You are only just starting to understand all that being a Christian entails. Quite frankly, it can be daunting to think about.

Next Sunday, look around the auditorium where you worship. Look for the older members, the ones who seemingly have it all figured out. Look for the ones that others turn to for advice, or who always seem to have the right answer in Bible Class, or a wise comment to add to whatever point the teacher is trying to make. Make a mental note of those people and then remember that many of them were, once upon a time, new Christians just like you are. They too started a new life in Christ with decades of living left to go. They have lots of answers to Bible questions today, but back then, they had all the same questions you have now.

What have I done? I'm a Christian now but what does that mean? I know what the preacher says; I can repeat the words, but I don't yet appreciate what it is I have pledged myself to follow. As the song says "I am mine no more: I've

been bought with blood and I am mine no more."
I'm a Christian now: What does that mean?

What have I *not* done? What hasn't
changed now that I'm a Christian? What
struggles and challenges did I live with, in blissful
ignorance, that are still present even as I belong
to Christ? What misconceptions are there about
becoming a Christian that are soon to slap me
right across the face? I'm a Christian now: What
does that *not* mean?

How do I say thanks to God? All I've
heard regarding my salvation is how undeserving
I am to receive it, and how unworthy I am to
love and die for, and yet Christ did those things
for me. It seems like such a small and inadequate
gesture, but how do I express my gratitude to
God for the salvation He gave me? I'm a
Christian now: How do I show my thankfulness?

How do I forgive myself? I did a lot of
things I now regret. I have to say "now regret"
because, the fact is, I didn't always regret them
back then. I did a lot of things I very much
enjoyed doing. Now that I'm a Christian, I look
back on what I did and I feel shame, even though
I'm promised by God that those shameful sins
have been washed away. I'm forgiven by God:
How do I forgive **myself**?

How do I be a disciple? So much time is
spent getting the lost to put on Christ in baptism.

WHAT NEXT?

As a preacher, I'll claim a profession-wide failing on our part: We need to spend as much time talking about **being** a Christian as we do **becoming** one. I've obeyed the Gospel, but that only means I'm now living a **life** of obedience. I'm a Christian now: How do I be a disciple?

What do I do with my old life? Becoming a Christian is often (rightly) described as putting to death the old "self" and being born again as a new "self." That illustration works as a metaphor, but in reality, I'm still the same me that I was ten seconds before I was put under the water. I have an entire life that I've lived thus far, with friends and loved ones orbiting around me who, unlike me, **didn't** make the decision to obey the Gospel. Unlike them, I'm a Christian now: What do I do with my old life?

When should I cut out bad influences? As said, I have a lot of people orbiting around me who aren't children of God. Everyone in my life is either going to be influenced by me or is going to be an influence on me. What do I do when some of those people that I hope to influence end up dragging me down, spiritually? I don't want to come up out of the water and immediately start defriending people on social media. Nevertheless, I **am** a Christian now: When should I cut out bad influences?

What if I sin? One of the reasons I gave my life to Christ was because I didn't want to go

8

to Hell. I was a sinner, lost in spirit, and on my way to eternal condemnation. I became a child of God to change that but now that I've been baptized, the Devil isn't going to leave me alone. On the contrary, he's coming after me even more intently than ever...and I'm not going to be able to fight him off every time. I'm going to slip up. What then? I'm a Christian now: What if I sin?

How do I deal with doubt? I know what I believed when I said "I'm ready to be baptized." I know what I confessed when I was asked "do you believe Jesus Christ is the Son of God?" But I will also admit that I sometimes wonder, sometimes question, and sometimes doubt. I live in a world that maintains almost a casual dismissal of everything the Bible teaches. I know I shouldn't think like that. I'm a Christian now: How do I deal with doubt?

How do I study and interpret the Bible? I'm not sitting around expecting God to whisper in my ear and tell me which way to turn at every fork in the road of life. I know I have to read the Bible to understand God's will. I also know that the Bible is a big book. Scratch that: It's sixty-six different big books all wrapped up together. I don't exactly know where to begin. I'm a Christian now: How do I study and interpret the Bible?

What is my "theology"? What do I say when people ask me what I believe? How do I go beyond

WHAT NEXT?

just a mindless regurgitation of a verse in the Bible to the point where I can explain the "why" of my faith? Lots of people can quote Scripture; even the Devil knows the Bible. What I want is to convert my knowledge of those words into a life-guiding worldview. I want to be able to know why I believe what I believe so that I can answer any challenge or attempt to shake my faith that comes my way. I'm a Christian now: What is my "theology"?

These different questions are likely to be asked, in one form or another, by new Christians everywhere. They deserve to be answered. You deserve to have them answered. New converts to Christ are, in many ways, the most vulnerable of God's people. While it's often the case that becoming a child of God brings with it a level of zeal and dedication that's hard to maintain over the years, it's also the case that the flame of zeal can quickly be extinguished by the first major obstacle that comes your way.

Be aware, Christian: The Devil has you in his sights. He will want to break you, to unsettle you, to shake your resolve, and to lead you away from your Master as soon as possible. You're a Christian now. What next? You have questions.

Let's answer them...

Chapter One

WHAT HAVE I DONE?

Countless people every year are taught the Gospel of Christ. In the USA, especially in the South, those people likely grew up having some kind of a "Christish" foundation already laid for them. Maybe they didn't go to church every Sunday or whisper a prayer before every meal, but if you asked them if they believed in God the answer would probably be *"yes."* If you asked who God's Son is, they'd probably tell you *"Jesus."*

If you ask them what to do to be saved...you probably would get a variety of different answers. Still, even then, the answers would probably end the same way: "...*That's what*

WHAT NEXT?

I believe but I'm not going to tell someone else that they're wrong if they don't believe the same way."

Our world and culture have become enamored with the idea that there is no single, identifiable "truth" to learn. People today talk about "your" truth and "my" truth as though the way you perceive something is the only objective standard to go by. If you hand someone a granny smith apple and ask them what color it is, regardless of what they say, the "true" answer does not change: The apple is green. Some things simply are what they are and do not change regardless of anyone's strong desire.

Becoming a Christian is about submitting to the authority of Jesus. It is to do things His way. Of course it is; faith requires reliance on someone else or it isn't faith at all. To put your trust and reliance in Jesus means submitting to His commands, whatever those commands may be. Does Jesus command one way to become a Christian to some people and another way to other people? No. There is only one way to be saved, which means all other ways are null and void.

When you understand that, you suddenly realize what becoming a Christian means: You have put yourself on an island, surrounded by people who have not done what you have done.

Actually, to be precise, it is not you that has put yourself on an island, but Jesus that has set you apart: He has called us out of darkness and placed us in His marvelous light (1 Peter 2:9). By obeying Him, by submitting to Him, by turning our lives over to Him, He has taken ownership over us.

Like a shepherd that finds a stray sheep, takes pity on it, and brings it home to live in a safe enclosure, the Lord found us when we were lost and astray. He took pity on us and brought us out of the wilderness to live with Him in His safe enclosure. That enclosure is His church. All who obey the Gospel are added to His church. There is no one in His church who hasn't obeyed the Gospel, and there is no one outside His church who has obeyed the Gospel.

You're a Christian now. Consider what that means. What have you done? That's a question usually asked with a negative connotation. When a parent enters the kitchen and sees a child standing over a mess of chocolate syrup and spilled ice cream, the question that follows is usually: "What have you done?!" When a teenager hears a parent shout their full name, first-middle-and-last, demanding they come downstairs, the question they usually

WHAT NEXT?

ask themselves, as they try to remember the past few hours, is "oh no, what have I done?"

This time, however, the question isn't negative. You haven't done anything bad. You've obeyed the Gospel. What you've done is something big. You've done something life-changing. You've done something that, hopefully, will alter the trajectory of your life from now until...forever.

There are many big moments that come to most people throughout their life, and all of them require a moment or two to consider the magnitude of it all. When I graduated High School, I sat around a campfire with a dozen others from my class thinking about the past thirteen years and how everything I had ever known—the morning routine, the classes, the tests, the homework, etc—was all about to go away (at the time I wasn't thinking about all the homework and tests that come with getting a Bachelor's and, later, a Master's Degree).

When I got married, I realized I would never be the same person again: I was no longer just "me," I was "my spouse and me." Her needs would now factor into every decision I would ever make. When each of my children were born I realized I was now responsible for the way a brand new human being would perceive the entire world around him.

MATTHEW L. MARTIN

It's good and healthy to pause and reflect as you approach a new chapter in your life. You've just become a Christian. What does that mean? How is that decision going to affect your life from now until the end? What have you done?

This question is not just one you're going to ask now, at the beginning of your Christian journey. It's one you might find yourself thinking about in twenty or thirty years, as you look back on the day you obeyed the Gospel. Many are the Christians who have said "I've been a Christian for twenty years and I worry sometimes if I did what I did for the right reasons."

The thing about becoming a Christian is that it's purely a spiritual process. As a result, there is no physical marking that a person can point to as an easy reminder of who they are. You can't say "I know I'm a Christian because I've got the scar to prove it right here..."

There is no physical identifier, so how do you know you're a Christian? The answer is "you know because you **know**." You know because you can read what the Word of God says and know that you did what it says. Even then, **all** we have, therefore, is a mental component, and that can be used by the Devil to stir up within us moments of disbelief. And it can make Christians

WHAT NEXT?

says to themselves, on occasion, "I know the date I was baptized, and I remember it happening, but in the years since then I don't feel like I'm living up to the standard of what I thought it meant to be a Christian." A Christian might wonder "did God even really save me back then, because I don't feel very saved right now..."

Those ideas all orbit around the question at the top of this chapter: "What have I done?" Whenever someone asks me about what they did when they became a Christian or if their salvation is still in effect, my answer to them is usually to turn their question around: "What **did** you do?"

Now let's understand that you didn't do anything to **earn** your salvation. Salvation is the result of God giving you and me something we did not deserve (Ephesians 2:8-9). In order to enjoy the gift of our salvation, God has given us commands to obey. So I can say "these are the things you have done to become a Christian" and I can list off things like: "You believed in God" and "you were baptized for the remission of sins," but none of those things bought your salvation. Your salvation was purchased by Christ's blood.

Really, the question "what have I done?" is the same as "What has God done for me?" because what you have done is allowed God to give you a gift you don't deserve. What does that look like?

When you became a Christian, you had your transgressions forgiven. Paul says "and you, being dead in your sins has God made to live with Him, having forgiven you all your trespasses" (Colossians 2:13).

To trespass is to go somewhere you're not supposed to go, or stand somewhere you're not supposed to be. Transgress is what you did to be a trespasser. The word "transgress" means "to step over a line." There is a boundary between where you're allowed to be and where you're not allowed to be, and if you step over that line you are a trespasser, because you have transgressed beyond the boundary God drew for you.

All of us have trespassed. We've said things we weren't supposed to say, thought things we weren't supposed to think, and done things we weren't supposed to do. We have all trespassed and gone beyond the holiness of God and made ourselves sinners. Those actions have consequences. According to Paul, those actions made us "dead in our sins."

But those transgressors, according to Paul, have been brought back to life by God. How? By being forgiven of their trespasses. You who were dead in your sins have, by the power and grace of God, been forgiven.

WHAT NEXT?

The trouble is, when you tell that to a Christian who is worrying about his spiritual relationship, he might say "that's great. I'm glad to know that God forgives sins when someone becomes a Christian...I'm just worried that He hasn't forgiven **me**!"

My answer to that would be: What did you do? What have you done? Did you do what Paul says? Were you "buried with Him in baptism and raised with Him through the faith of the operation of God" (Colossians 2:12)?

If you wonder if God forgave you, just ask yourself if you did what He said to do to **be** forgiven? Were you buried with Christ in baptism? If you were then stop worrying about what **you** did and have faith in what God says **He** did. When you are baptized, according to Paul, God operates on your soul, like a surgeon cutting a cancerous tumor away from a patient. God removes the sin from your soul and brings you to life again. Unlike a surgery to remove a tumor, however, there is no scar to prove you were operated on by God. Instead, you have faith and trust that God performed the operation and that it was a success.

Look at it this way, if God failed to remove your sins then it's God who failed, not you, and if God failed you're doomed anyway! But if you believe, as I'm sure you do, that God cannot fail, then trust Him: You were baptized according to His commands (Mark 16:16), and He saves those who are.

The Devil is a liar and a skillful one at that. He will lie to you and convince you that it is you that has the burden of proof concerning your salvation. And you, lacking any physical evidence, will fret and worry and begin to question. These questions will only get worse as you inevitably stumble into sin long after the water from the baptistry has dried off (we'll talk more about that in chapter eight).

Don't let the lying Devil frame the issue that way. It's not you that has the burden of proof, but God. Again, you're not the Savior; God is. You're not the one buying your salvation; Jehovah bought it and offered it to you as a gift. Are there conditions connected to that gift? Yes! The Lord sets the terms: "Believe and be baptized," He says (Mark 16:16). Those are conditions. "Take up your cross and follow Me," He says (Matthew 16:24). That's a condition. But those are **His** conditions, not yours.

Did you believe Jesus would save you when you were baptized? Did you agree to follow Him as a servant follows a master? I'm not asking if you have followed Him perfectly since then. I'm not asking if your trust in Him has been 100% unwavering since then. I'm asking when you

WHAT NEXT?

obeyed the Gospel did you give your life to Christ for Him to save? If you did then trust that He saved you.

You're a Christian now. What have you done? You have had your sins washed away. There's a lot more that goes into it than that, but that's the starting point. You've become a brand new person. You've started over. And even though you will make mistakes and sometimes completely fall back into the ditch, the fact that you **are** a Christian will never change, and the way back to His forgiving arms will always be open to you.

It's a scary world you're living in, physically. For all your life, this world has been full of people who weren't saved, many of whom were outright hostile toward Christ. The world still is that way; the difference is you: You are now saved. You belong to a new and better spiritual world, but physically you're still living in this place where you are surrounded by people who no longer think like you, talk like you, or do the things you do. Those people might even be outright hostile toward you, just as they are toward your Master. So be it. Let them. You know what you have done.

You have been saved.

Chapter Two

WHAT HAVE I *NOT* DONE?

There are countless misconceptions that people have about becoming a Christian, being a Christian, or staying a Christian. It's common even for the one making the big decision to go into it with misconceptions, too. As much as everyone is studying with you and helping you along the way, no teacher can anticipate every possible question a person might have.

What's more, while preachers often talk about how important it is for a baptized person to know what they're doing before they are immersed, the fact is no one can account for the questions they didn't know to ask. We're not talking about someone being baptized who actively believes the wrong thing; we're talking about being baptized while assuming something is right when it is actually wrong.

Rest assured, these false assumptions do not nullify or cancel out the saving power of God. I have talked to many people and taught many classes with people who have been Christians for a year, or five years, or a decade, or sometimes longer, who will make comments and remarks about what it means to be a Christian (or what it doesn't mean) that are entirely out of step with what the New Testament teaches. They're not false teachers; they're people who didn't know and didn't know to ask.

Becoming a Christian requires certain things of you. Likewise, when you become a Christian, God accomplishes certain things in you. On the other hand, there are many things that do not happen. There are many things that some might even assume happen, which absolutely do not.

You're a Christian now: What have you *not* done? To start with, you have not joined a denomination. What is a denomination? In the religious context, it is an organization of religious observers, who adhere to a particular doctrine, leadership structure, and system of government.

MATTHEW L. MARTIN

Denominations are organizations founded by various people, who set themselves apart from other denominations by their name, their practices, and their particular beliefs.

For example, you can tell the difference between a Methodist and a Baptist in how they administer a baptism: The former sprinkles its members with water while the latter immerses its members into water. You can tell the Catholic Church is distinct from the others in that they have a class of priests who are separated from the rest of the members.

And so on.

Who decided for the Methodists that baptism was a sprinkling? The leadership of the Methodist church made the ruling. That leadership traces back to the Anglican priest John Wesley who founded the denomination in the late 1700s.

Who decided Catholic priests would wear black suits with the little white patch under their adam's apple, would never marry, and would always be Irish in movies from the 1970s? The leadership of the Catholic church made the ruling. That leadership is a pyramid with the Pope at the top, an office that has been around in one form or another since at least the 600s, with some aspects going back as far as the 300s.

WHAT NEXT?

The point is, when people start deciding how they are going to worship, how they are going to be organized, and what they are going to believe, you will always end up with division. People, almost by nature, tend not to get along. We disagree, we argue and, when both sides think they have the right way to do something, we either go to war or we go our separate ways and do our own things.

Religious division—even so-called "Christian religious division"—is so commonplace in the world today that most don't even consider it a problem anymore. People take it as a given that there are different churches that teach different things to accommodate different people. This is not the way of Christ, however.

Our Master wants unity of the believers (John 17:20-21). His inspired Apostles command us to believe and speak the same things, that there be no divisions among us, and that we come to the same conclusions as brethren should (1 Corinthians 1:10).

When a person becomes a Baptist, he does so by adhering to the rules and regulations laid down by the Baptist Church, an entity founded by, run by, and maintained by flawed people. When a person becomes a Methodist, he does so by agreeing to follow the customs and laws that define someone *as* a Methodist. Those laws were written by flawed people.

When you strip away the doctrines written by Baptists and Methodist, Presbyterians, Catholics, Pentecostals, and the like, and you just take and obey the Bible, what do you have? To become a Baptist one must take the Bible in one hand and the tenets of the Baptist church in the other. What happens if you just take the Bible in both hands? What do you become then?

When you obey the Gospel, as written in the New Testament, you become a Christian. That's it. You don't become a *kind* of Christian. You just become a Christian. Whenever someone asks me what my religion is, I answer "Christian." When they ask me what kind of Christian, I answer, "a faithful one." On the other hand, I could get a little more specific if I wanted...

You are a Christian now. What kind of Christian are you? You're a CATHOLIC Christian. It's true. Now, granted, you're not a Roman Catholic Christian because you don't follow Roman Catholic doctrine. You only follow the Bible, and the Bible makes Christians that are "catholic."

The word "catholic" means "universal." You are a universal Christian, which means no matter where you go, no matter who you are around, you will be a child of God. You don't

WHAT NEXT?

have to bend your beliefs to accommodate any other person or religious group. You are what you are. You are what Christ made you. You are a universal (catholic) Christian.

You are also a BAPTIST Christian. You are not a member of the Baptist denomination, which began in 1609 by a man named John Smyth. You are a Christian, and a member of the church Jesus Himself established and rules over as King. You are "baptist" in your belief, however, because you were baptized and you will tell others of the importance of baptism, too.

We can go on like this, talking about how you are "methodist" in your beliefs, because you adhere to the method and pattern laid down in the New Testament for how a Christian should live. You are also "pentecostal," in that you belong to the church that was established on the Pentecost holiday following the Lord's ascension into Heaven (Acts 2). You are also "presbyterian" in that you submit to a body of elders (presbyters) who watch out for you under God's command (Acts 20:28).

The point is when you became a Christian you did not join a denomination. You became part of something that predates all man-made religious division of Christianity. You were baptized into and became part of the body of Jesus Christ (1 Corinthians 12:13).

MATTHEW L. MARTIN

You may attend a weekly worship service at a building with a sign out front that says "CHURCH OF CHRIST," but that does not make you part of a denomination. A sign to tell people who you are does not make you a denomination. As said, denominations are organizations founded by various people, and set themselves apart from other denominations by their name, their practices, and their particular beliefs.

The church of Jesus Christ is set apart by our practices and beliefs, but who set us apart? Who founded the church of Christ? Who established the church that is talked about in the New Testament? What church is that? Is it the Baptist church that we read about in Acts? Is Paul writing to the Corinthian Methodist Church? Was the church at Ephesus the same as the Presbyterian Church that's down the road from where you live? No. No. No again.

Jesus saved you, and by saving you He set you apart from those who are not saved. Being set apart is the same as being part of His church. The word "church" even means "those who are called out." What you did was obey Jesus, and be added by Jesus to the church that belongs to Jesus. What you did **not** do was join a religious club founded by flawed people, and distinct from other religious clubs founded by flawed people in the way that all opinions of men are distinct.

WHAT NEXT?

Speaking of flawed people, something else you did not do when you became a Christian was make yourself better than everyone else. To be set apart is to be separated from the lost, but that separation is not because you are so great. It is because God desires His people to be distinct from the rest of the world. That was true of the physical nation of Israel in the Old Testament, when God ordered them not to follow the customs and practices of the pagan nations around them, but to be "holy" as He is holy (Leviticus 19).

That same principle is true today: Christians are a people made holy by God. We are His holy nation of saved people (1 Peter 2:9). That does not make us better than anyone. As one of my preacher-heroes Bob Turner often said: "We are not better than the lost: Christ is better. Christ is the Savior. What we are is better *off* than the lost. We have a Heavenly hope that the lost do not have."

Because we are not better than the lost, and because we have something greater than the lost, we ought to have a great desire to talk to the lost, to try and help them attain the same salvation that we did, so that they can be "better off" as we are.

Do not look down on the lost. Remember that you were once as they are, and remember also that you can give them the same words you were given, which can help them know what to do to be saved, too (Acts 11:13-14).

Speaking of Christ as the Savior, something else you did not do was earn your salvation. Were there commands you had to obey? Yes, but obeying them did not put God in your debt. At no point were you able to say to God "now you owe **me**." On the contrary, Christ is innocent and we were guilty. We sinned. We deserved to go to Hell forevermore.

The only reason we are saved is because Christ wanted us to be. Had he not, He would not have come from Heaven to Earth. He would have left us to rot in our transgressions and die in spiritual depravity.

And yet, in order for us to be saved—to take advantage of the mercy and love He extended toward us—we had to obey certain commands. What baffles my mind is how some people will hear that and think "if you have to do something for the reward, that means you earn the reward," as if salvation is a paycheck and baptism is the 9-to-5 job we just worked for it.

No. Baptism is not a job. Baptism is a command. Salvation is not a paycheck. Salvation is a reward. Instead of thinking of it like a job, think of it as a gift, because that's how the New

WHAT NEXT?

Testament describes salvation: Paul says we are "saved by grace through faith, not by ourselves; it is a gift of God" (Ephesians 2:8).

Imagine you had a physical illness and someone said to you that they had a pill you could swallow that would take the illness away. All you have to do is take the pill, pop it in, down some water, and be healed. Would you do it? I think you would.

Does taking the pill as prescribed in any way earn your healing? Did you create the medicine? Did you manufacture it in pill form? Did you distribute it to the masses of sick people? Did you do any of the work? No. All you did was obey the doctor's orders.

How does obeying an order equal earning salvation? If I earn salvation then I am saying to God "you must save me." I'm giving the order. I'm calling the shots. He is the servant and I am the master. That's not how it works. In reality, He is the Master and I am the servant. He told me I deserved to die but, if I obey Him I will be saved.

It takes faith to obey, but it is grace that saves (again, Ephesians 2:8). Don't let anyone tell you that you think you earned your salvation by being baptized. You didn't earn anything; you obeyed a command (Mark 16:16). The question ought to be why someone who wants to be saved and to serve Jesus would start that process by refusing to obey the commands of Jesus!

Ask the person who would dare say that to you what **they** had to do to be saved. While there are some people out there who believe Jesus decides who is lost and who is saved and we have no say in the matter at all, the vast majority of people who acknowledge Jesus is the Savior also believe a person must do **something** to be saved, whether that something is "ask Jesus to come into your heart" or "say the sinner's prayer" or "just believe." Whatever it is, most will say you must do something.

What must you do? If they say "believe" then point out to them that, based on their logic, they think they are earning their salvation, because "believe" is something a person must do. The fact is, the problem with those people is not that you must do something, it's what you're saying they must do. Those people don't want to be baptized for the remission of sins as the New Testament commands (Acts 2:38). They want to believe, only believe, and nothing else. But they don't say that; they say "you're trying to earn your salvation" or "work your way to Heaven." In truth, you're just obeying the Master.

Naaman was a man doomed to die of leprosy. He was told he could be healed if he had faith enough to dip in the waters of the Jordan

WHAT NEXT?

River. He obeyed. He was healed. He did not earn his salvation. It was a gift (2 Kings 5).

You were a person doomed to die in your sins. You were told you could be healed if you had faith enough to be baptized. You obeyed. You were healed. You did not earn your salvation. It was a gift.

We sinned. We deserve to go to Hell. Salvation is not about giving us what we deserve; it's about giving us what we don't...at the expense of Christ, who died on the cross, suffering what He didn't deserve, so that we would not have to suffer what we **did** deserve.

And speaking of our sinful past, the last thing you did **not** do when you became a Christian was erase your past. To be clear, as far as God is concerned, your sins are washed away and He does not bring them to mind anymore (Hebrews 8:12). On the other hand, God does not change the past when you become a Christian.

You **were** a sinner. You always will **have been** a sinner. Your past cannot be changed but it is simply not held against you by the Eternal Judge. At the end of the day, that's all that matters. In the meantime, however, you may have to deal with and live with the consequences of your past mistakes. God is forgiving. The IRS might not be. Many people on Death Row have turned to Christ and found salvation...and then died as punishment for their crimes a few days later.

Many people lived hard and cruel lives before finding Christ. They made many enemies. They hurt many people. It can be hard for others to see you in a different way now that you have found Christ. You have been saved; maybe they haven't. And maybe your past misdeeds were so terrible that your new life in Christ might end up turning them **away** from Jesus. That's not fair, but that does happen.

Even the Apostle Paul, who once was a persecutor of the church, found many of his new brethren in Christ did not initially trust him (Acts 9:26). Paul's past sins were washed away, but the memories of the people he hurt were not. It can be discouraging, but stay positive: Know who you are and remember what you've done to make your wrongs right.

You're a Christian now. You know what that means. Meditate on what it doesn't mean: You did not join a religious group founded by men; you were added to a spiritual body overseen by Jesus.

You did not become superior to anyone in the world; you became set apart from the world and have an obligation now to help others be set apart with you.

WHAT NEXT?

You did not earn your salvation; it was a gift Jesus paid for, which you accepted through obedience to His commands.

And you did not unburden yourself from the way the rest of the world will think of you as a result of your past. You have, however, been set free from the Divine punishment of your past actions, and when it comes time for judgment, the opinions and feelings of other people will not matter a bit.

Chapter Three

HOW DO I SAY
"THANKS" TO GOD?

Ordinarily, a person might not think twice about saying "thank you." By that, I mean it should be so ingrained in us as decent people that, whenever someone does anything even remotely kind to us, we are compelled to say "thanks." Is it possible that the one being to whom we ought to be the most grateful is the one we think to say "thanks" to the least?

I did a quick skim through the Gospel record, examining every miracle which Jesus did in order to help someone else directly. In other words, I didn't consider miracles like His walking on water or when He gave Simon more fish than

WHAT NEXT?

his net could handle. Instead, I looked at healing miracles. In all, there are thirty-one occasions wherein Jesus performed a miracle that specifically helped someone in need, whether they were hungry, injured, sick, or even dead.

In all those times, do you know how many instances feature the one who received help saying "thank you" to God?

Once.

Keep in mind, you can find numerous examples of God's people in the Old Testament expressing gratitude in poetic forms. You can also find times in the New Testament when the Lord's people "gave thanks" for their meal. What you don't find, but for one time, are examples of people being directly blessed by Jesus and, upon receiving the blessing, saying "thank you" to the Miracle Man.

That doesn't mean those people did not say thank you in some way. It could be that their gratitude was expressed by not recorded by the writers. Also, that's not to say those people weren't thankful. But, still, I find it interesting that only once is it ever recorded where a person said "thank you" to Jesus. That one instance is the only example of a "thank you" to God until you get to the epistles: Paul, for example, says some variation of "thanks be to God" in almost every book he wrote, sometimes multiple times per book.

But that's not really what we think of when we talk about "saying thank you." When we hear those words, we mean expressing gratitude in the immediate aftermath of an act of kindness. In that case, the pickings in the New Testament are woefully slim.

So here's a chapter that, based on what you've just read, might seem like it will have no Biblical source material to draw from. On the contrary, while we don't have more than a single example of someone saying "thank you," we do have examples of people demonstrating their thankfulness in one way or another.

John records a miracle in which Jesus healed the son of a nobleman of Capernaum, whose son was sick to the point of death. The Lord told the man to return to his son, assuring him that his child would live. Sure enough, when the nobleman returned home, he found his son safe and sound. In response, John writes that the nobleman believed on the Lord "with all his house" (John 4:46-53). How did this person express his gratitude to Jesus? He did so by leading his family, as the head of his house, into faith and reliance on Jesus.

WHAT NEXT?

Another example is found in Matthew's writing, which tells of two blind men who begged the Lord for healing (Matthew 9:27-31). In response, Jesus touched them and gave them back their sigh. After they were healed, the Lord asked them not to proclaim what He had done. Why not? We can only speculate, but perhaps it has something to do with what He said in His sermon on the mount, about not being showy with your righteous acts (Matthew 6:1-4). On the other hand, maybe He had things to do and didn't want to be swarmed by people at that time.

Either way, as soon as the healed men left Jesus, the first thing they did was run and tell everybody what He had done for them. Obviously, this is disobedience, but we can at least understand why they did it: They were so full of joy and thankfulness they just wanted everyone to know what the Lord had done for them. It may be disobedient, but it's **grateful** disobedience, nonetheless.

Speaking of blind men, there is another example of Jesus meeting and healing blind men: Matthew mentions people shouting at Him from a crowd, begging for mercy. When Jesus asked what they wanted from Him, they did not mince words; they asked to have their eyes opened. Jesus then touched their eyes and made them free to see. In response, though they did not say "thank you," they did drop everything and follow Him (Matthew 20:30-34). Their actions expressed their gratitude, as did the actions of the previous blind men, and the nobleman whose son was healed.

Still, that's only three examples out of thirty or so miracles we have recorded. Only three times do we find people demonstrating gratitude. Maybe it doesn't matter. Maybe Jesus didn't care whether or not the people He healed said thank you. Could that be?

I don't think so.

Remember, there is one time recorded when someone went back to tell Jesus thank you: The Lord had just healed ten lepers. Nine of them went on their merry way; one of them returned to the Master, fell down at Jesus' feet, and thanked Him (Luke 17:12-17).

Jesus' response to this one thankful leper is notable: He said "Ten were cleansed...where are the nine?" Based on His words, I don't think it's out of line to say Jesus cares about whether or not we are thankful for what He does for us.

On another occasion, Jesus fed five thousand men (plus women and children). The next day they all went looking for Him. When they found Him, the Lord rebuked them, saying they were not interested in His teaching, only in being fed. They were not genuinely thankful as a

WHAT NEXT?

sincere-hearted person would be when blessed by God. Had they been, they would have done as the nobleman did: They would have believed on Him. Had they been thankful, they would have done as the blind men did: They would have followed Him as Disciples. Had they been thankful, they would have done as the one leper did: They would have given thanks to God.

With all that said, we return to the original question of the chapter. We must say thank you to God. He has saved us, despite our supreme unworthiness. We owe Him infinite gratitude. How fortunate are we that His salvation will provide us with infinite heavenly opportunities to be thankful?!

In the meantime, we must answer the question at the top of the chapter: How do we say "thank you" to God? As said, it's commonplace for us to say thank you to regular people when they do something nice to us. Thanking God for something as monumental as sending Jesus to die for our sins feels almost too big for a simple "thank you."

What can we do?

The words of Paul provide a wonderful template for daily Christian living. It's one of the great blessings of his many epistles; they are overflowing with many practical statements we can apply to our lives to better our walk with Christ. To that end, the Apostle wrote some things to the Colossian church that we can use to answer this question...

SAY IT:

*And let the peace of God rule in your hearts, to the which also ye are called in one body; and be ye thankful (**Colossians 3:15**).*

SING IT:

*Let the word of Christ dwell in you richly in all wisdom; teaching and admonishing one another in psalms and hymns and spiritual songs, singing with thankfulness in your hearts to the Lord (**Colossians 3:16**).*

SHOW IT:

*And whatsoever ye do in word or deed, do all in the name of the Lord Jesus, giving thanks to God and the Father by him (**Colossians 3:17**).*

The above verses occur, in order, one after the other, but I broke them up into individual

WHAT NEXT?

readings because each verse offers a different answer to the question of the chapter.

How do we say thank you to God? To start with, we just "say" thank you. As Paul says in Colossians 3:15: "be ye thankful." That's it. Don't overthink it. Don't be so overwhelmed by the magnitude of the gift that you feel a simple "thank you" is inadequate. Sure, if all you ever did was say "thanks," and your life never changed, that would be an inadequate response, but this is just the first step.

There is power in words. More than just thinking thankful thoughts, we must vocalize our gratitude. Whether that means telling others how thankful we are, as the blind men did (despite being asked not to by the Lord), or whispering our thanks to the Lord in prayer, just saying the words is enough to remind us what was done for us.

If history, as recorded in the Bible, tells us anything, it is that people are tremendously adept at forgetting about God and His blessings. On the other hand, talking about them is a surefire way to ensure we do not forget, nor take them for granted.

Paul described in great detail all the ways the Gentile world fell into godlessness, and he put a cap on it by saying "neither were they thankful" (Romans 1:21). Once the people lost their sense of gratitude, they took God's blessings for granted. What followed was their serving creation over Creator.

We are saved. We should be thankful for it. Paul tells us in Colossians 3 to say so: Be ye thankful.

Not only should we say it but we should sing it, too. That's what Paul says: "Sing with thankfulness in your hearts" (Colossians 3:16). Some translations say to sing with "grace," but most use the word "gratitude" or "thanksgiving." The idea is the same: Our singing should be a gift we give back to God as a thank you for the salvation He gave us.

Do our hymns compare to His salvation? Not at all, but we can't give a gift that's comparable to salvation, and God doesn't ask us to try: He asks us (in this verse) to sing with grateful hearts. So, even if it's the least I can do, I will do it, because it's the least I can do.

What do my hymns sound like? Are they lethargic? Do I mumble through them in disinterest? Do I treat the singing portion of worship as a time to talk to the person next to me in the pew, check my phone, or go get a drink of water? Is singing an optional thing we get to decline to participate in if we don't like the sound of our voice?

WHAT NEXT?

Many Christians sit silently during the singing of hymns, staring at the words on the page or on the screen but uttering not a sound. Why? If you ask them they will say "I don't know the song" or "I don't like to sing."

Setting aside the fact that singing is a command from God that we are obligated to obey (and therefore isn't dependent on whether or not we like doing it), Paul specifically frames the action as an act of gratitude. If a Christian doesn't know the song, that Christian should learn the song. Is that too much to ask? I think some would balk at that idea, but those who do are selfish.

Christians that would rather refuse to give God a gift than give Him one they feel isn't "good enough" are Christians too concerned with how their gifts might look (or sound) to others than they are with simply being thankful to God for His incredible gift.

So you have a terrible voice. Fine. Who cares? Are you worshipping the bratty teenager sitting in front of you, or are you worshipping God? Who died for your soul? Sing to Him; He doesn't care what it sounds like. If you don't know the song, then muddle along as best you can until you do.

It's funny how a person can listen to a new song from their favorite artist, not know any of the words, and sing along anyway: The words are almost always completely wrong, but who cares: If you want to sing, you'll give it your all and eventually learn it as you go. If we can do that with pop music, we can do that with hymns. And if we care enough to learn the words to a pop song and we don't care enough to do the same with our hymns, we can hardly be called grateful people.

Do you want to be thankful? Do you want to say thank you to God? Say it. Sing it.

Show it...

Paul says for our words and deeds to be in the name of Jesus (by His authority), as we "give thanks to the Father." In other words, not only should our every action reflect our life in Christ but, according to the Apostle, everything we do should be able to be interpreted as an act of gratitude to God.

When I give food to a beggar on the street, it's not because I want to appear altruistic to anyone watching; it's because I was once spiritually destitute, and God gave me Living Water to drink. I'm thankful for that, so helping a person with their worldly needs is a way to express my gratitude to God for what He did for me.

WHAT NEXT?

When I visit someone who is sick, it's not because I want to score brownie points. It's because I was once dying, and Jesus left Heaven to visit me, teach me, and die instead me. When I visit others, it's a way to emulate what my Master did for me. I'm thankful He came for me, so I go to others.

Listen to the things Jesus focuses on when describing the separation of sheep from goats (Matthew 25): The people who will depart from Him aren't singled out as murderers, rapists, thieves, or lewd people. The people He singles out are those who wouldn't feed the hungry or visit the needy. It's the people who won't do as He did, who won't follow His example, that are called out and condemned.

The Lord showed us how much He loved us through all the things He did for us. What better way to say thank you than to show Him how grateful we are for the new life He gave us? And what better way to do that than to live that new life as He lived His own?

You're a Christian now. You're not condemned; you're saved. Aren't you thankful? Of course you are.

Say it.
Sing it.
Show it.

Chapter Four

HOW DO I FORGIVE MYSELF?

Before getting to the question of the chapter, consider the sheer magnitude of the sacrifice of Christ. Consider not only the toll He went through in being betrayed, scourged, mocked, and nailed to a cross, but consider also the fact that He endured all of those things of His own volition. He died willingly. He could have called twelve legions of angels at any point during His suffering and ended it all, yet He did not. Why? Why would anyone willingly suffer as He did?

He suffered as a sacrifice, dying for us. He paid the ultimate price and took on the

WHAT NEXT?

punishment that we deserved in order to spare us from suffering it. He endured the mockery that He did not deserve, in order to save us from the penalty due for the crimes we had done.

Consider also the fact that, while some people in the world do not care at all that Jesus died for them, others have soft hearts that are easily touched by the story of Jesus. Some, however, have hearts that are so tender and so guilt-stricken that, when confronted with the Gospel message, instead of running to Jesus to be freed from their guilt, they resist the offer of salvation.

Why would someone touched by the message reject the invitation to be saved from their past? For some, their guilt is such an ingrained part of their life, they don't know how to cope with the idea that their past misdeeds can be removed. Some are so burdened, hating themselves so much over mistakes they made that they don't feel worthy to have their sins taken away.

If you think that's an unlikely scenario, you are mistaken. I have personally talked with and counselled people exactly like that. Many of them went on to become Christians. What kind of struggles do you imagine a Christian has to deal with who has that kind of mindset?

I remember being a brand-new Christian in High School and striking up a semi-friendship with someone a year older than me. I say "semi-friendship" because we had almost nothing in common, but we shared mutual friends. We were friends-in-law, let's say.

This person was a Christian, my brother in Christ, but he was hardly faithful. He would admit as such. In fact, he did admit it, many times. He would call me, usually late on Sunday, wanting to tell me all of the things he had done that weekend. Keep in mind, we were living in the middle-of-nowhere Arkansas, and yet he was doing things that I didn't even know you could get access to where we lived.

So there I would be: Listening to this person confess to me all their sins, and not any sins he had done against me, but just sins he had committed, sins I didn't need to know about in such detail. Still, he needed an ear, and he needed someone to pray for him, and I was happy to help. I would listen and then, when he was done, I would pray with him over the phone that he would resist temptation, draw closer to Christ, and be forgiven of his sins.

I don't know if he knew about James 5:16, and the writer's admonition for us to "confess our sins to each other and pray for each other" but that's the verse I kept thinking of every time he called. And he called a bunch.

Eventually, I came to understand why it was happening, and why he seemed so

WHAT NEXT?

unconfident in his own prayers to God that he needed me to offer some of my own for him: This person was drowning so deeply in the pit of sin that he did not believe God could (or would) hear his prayers anymore. He thought I had a better shot getting through to God than he did, despite the fact that I was struggling with plenty of my own sins, let me tell you.

Actually no, I won't tell you.

This friend of mine was a person who did not believe God would forgive him. I could hear it in his voice, every Sunday night when he would call me, finally clear-headed enough to grasp the consequences of his actions. The problem for him was, though he would express sorrow over his actions, and though he would express fear over the consequences of his actions, and though he would repent and be forgiven...he would never forgive himself.

What happens to a Christian who can't forgive himself? What happens when you believe, no matter what, that you are unworthy of salvation? Despite having a tender heart that regrets sinning, a person who believes he is incapable of being forgiven is a person that will fall into a life of sinful activity. After al, why not? If a person can't be forgiven then all they can do is chase the temporary pleasure that comes with iniquity.

Being a Christian who is able to forgive himself is not just good therapy; it's necessary to maintain a healthy relationship with God. How do we do it? How does someone who hates his past so much he refuses to let go of it finally relent and turn loose of all the things which God has already forgiven?

Knowing the answer is easy, but that doesn't mean it is easily done. The answer is this: You have to have faith. On one occasion, a man whose son was possessed with a demon came to the Lord, asking for help. In the midst of their conversation, he cried out: "Lord I believe; help my unbelief" (Mark 9:23).

The statement seems contradictory: Does he believe or not? He says he does, so why does he need help? I think the man's words are an acknowledgment of the need for growth. "I do have faith but I also need more faith tomorrow than I have today. And I'll need more the day after that than I will have tomorrow."

Far from a statement of weakness, the man utters exactly the kind of humble words Jesus is looking for. The man knew he was too weak to help his son, but he also knew Jesus was strong enough. He believed in the big picture that Jesus could help, but he had many doubts and uncertainties about the little things. He knew he had a daily struggle ahead of him to overcome those little doubts, one at a time.

Forgiving yourself is not a one-day fix. It is a daily struggle that may or may not get easier with time. It begins, however, with faith. Specifically, it begins in the faith of the operation of God. That's how Paul describes our salvation to the Colossians...

> *Buried with him in baptism, wherein also ye are risen with him through the faith of the operation of God, who hath raised him from the dead (***Colossians 2:12***).*

As mentioned in the book's introduction, When we become a Christian, other than getting wet, we are, on the outside, the same person that went into the water as we were when I came out of the water. The change occurs not to our physical body, but to our spiritual.

And yet, because we have no physical evidence to point to regarding our salvation, no scars or distinguishing markers we can hold up to others (or ourselves) and say "look, I'm saved; I've got the scar to prove it," it can be hard for some to believe it's real. Thus, we rely on something that makes the unseen real: Faith provides the evidence for what is unseen (Hebrews 11:1). We walk by faith because we don't have to walk by sight (2 Corinthians 5:7). We believe that God operated on our souls and cut the cancerous sin away from our spiritual bodies, because He told us He did, and we trust Him never to lie to us.

Jeremiah the prophet said that the saved would have their sins "remembered no more" (Jeremiah 31:34). A person may have great guilt over their sin, and because of that, the memories of their past mistakes may haunt their thoughts, but here's the good news: You can't hold yourself accountable for the sins that God has forgiven. You can't condemn yourself for a crime that God "remembers no more."

How does God forget? That's what the prophet says: God "remembers our sins no more." How does God, with His perfect, infinite mind, not "remember" all that we have done? In point of fact, He does. God knows everything we ever did. By that definition, He absolutely "remembers" our sins. What God doesn't do is "hold us accountable" for those sins anymore.

It's like how, in a courtroom, when the prosecutor says something about the defendant that was against the rules, the Judge will instruct the jury to disregard what was said and not use it in their deliberations. So, even though the jury

WHAT NEXT?

heard what was said, they're not allowed to use it against the person on trial: It might as well not have been said.

God "remembers no more" our sins in the sense that He "does not bring them up again." God does not tell His mind to recall them and, when we stand in Judgment one day, we will not hear about them. Though the Devil—the accuser—will try and bring them up, Jesus—our defense attorney (1 John 2:1)—will quickly interject and say "those crimes have been stricken from the record, washed away by My blood."

You may hate your past, but your past can't hurt you anymore unless you let it. Only you can bring your past to mind, and only you can let it draw you away from God. So, instead of fretting over the crimes you did before you were saved, and instead of letting guilt lead you to believe you are unworthy of the salvation you already have (and cannot lose as long as you are faithful), why not have faith, and trust that God will do as He's promised?

Trust that God has saved you. Trust that God will save you in the end. Recognize that a lack of faith in your salvation implies a lack of trust in the effectiveness of the Cross. Is Christ the Savior or isn't He? Is His blood effective or isn't it? Can a person be forgiven or can't he? If you insist on beating yourself up with guilt, then let me beat you up a little, too: Take this as a measure of tough love...

Get over yourself.

You're not special. You're not the one person that Jesus is unable to save. You're not a sinner any worse than the worst sinner God has ever seen, and He's seen worse than you.

Jesus saved Paul, a murderous, hate-filled, persecutor of Christians. Jesus saved Peter, a man who—at the exact moment Jesus was telling the High Priest "go ask my Disciples about Me; they'll tell you who I am"—was sitting by a fire while people did exactly that, asking him about Jesus. What did Peter do? He denied even knowing Jesus.

The Lord saved a murderous thief hanging next to Him on the cross, a man who, a few hours earlier, was joining in with the mob below in mocking His Divinity. And speaking of that mob, while Jesus was hanging on the cross, the priests and leaders below Him were hurling all manner of vicious insults at Him. What did He say to God about them? "Father forgive them." Are you worse than they? Even if you were, Jesus still died for you, too.

Paul once referred to himself as the "chief of sinners." Do you think he struggled with guilty

WHAT NEXT?

feelings regarding his past? I do. Nevertheless, in that same statement, the Apostle remarked that it was for sinners like him that Jesus came to save (1 Timothy 1:15). And that same Paul—chief of sinners he believed himself to be—at the end of his life, spoke with assurance (faith) that he had a crown of life waiting for him on the other side of death (2 Timothy 4:8).

Remember, the feeling of guilt and the struggle with forgiving yourself is entirely a "you" problem. It's not a "God" problem. He **has** forgiven you. Through Him, you have conquered the Devil. The danger comes when you let the Devil continue to whisper, like the sore loser he is, in your ear.

Who do you think benefits from you refusing to forgive yourself? Does God benefit? No: He is robbed of a hard worker in His Kingdom. Do you benefit? No: You linger in spiritual lethargy, unable to rise to a new level of faithfulness because you keep feeling unworthy. Who is it that benefits from you refusing to forgive yourself?

The devil. So do what James said: "Resist the Devil and He will flee from you" (James 4:7). How do you do that? James tells you in the very next verse: "Draw near to God and He will draw near to you" (James 4:8). The Devil hates God.

He hates when God is present in someone's life. And don't think for a second that he's not clever enough or cruel enough to use your own tender heart and guilt against you.

The way to overcome a struggle with forgiving self is through faith, and faith comes by hearing the Word of God (Romans 10:17). So, when we study God's Word, we reinforce in our minds the confidence that God operated on us and saved us from our sins. As we do, the Devil naturally flees from us, because he can't stand it when God's people read their Bibles.

And as the Devil distances himself from you, so too will the lingering thoughts about your supposed unworthiness to enjoy the blessing of salvation. The whispers in your ear that you don't deserve to be saved and that you should give up will fizzle away, because they were only ever lies told to you by the Devil.

The fact is, you may struggle with these negative thoughts for years. Truth be told, you may **always** struggle with them. Unfortunately, I can't change that, and there is no quick and simple formula you can follow to make it go away instantly and never return.

Not every Christian is going to have this problem, but I know for a fact that, if you do, you are not the only one who does. Other brethren will have their own—different—

WHAT NEXT?

hardships they will deal with as children of God. That's just part of living in this sinful world.

The Lord has called us to take up our cross and follow Him (Luke 9:23). We all have our crosses to bear. We all have our thorns in the flesh to contend with. The Master never promised life with Him would be easy. He said it is easier than whatever the world offers (Matthew 11:28-30). He never promised it would be "easy;" He promised it would be "worth it."

Rest assured, you are saved. And even in your darkest day, when that fact seems impossible, know that it is not. You can take it for certain that Christ is your Friend, your Savior, and your Judge who will one day invite you—saved and forgiven—to enter into eternal joy (Matthew 25:21) as a faithful child of the King.

Chapter Five

HOW DO I BE A DISCIPLE?

Becoming a Christian isn't like learning a skill, nor is being a Christian akin to having a skill. It's not something you take up and do for a while, mastering it with practice, so that when the right moment comes, you can perform or demonstrate or somehow put your newfound skill to good use. Christianity isn't a well-developed hobby; Christianity is a life.

You have died and risen again. There's nothing "part-time" about that, and there is no "right" moment to demonstrate Christianity because every moment for the rest of your life is a moment in which you will **be** a Christian. You never know when the life you live will be an

WHAT NEXT?

influence, either positively or negatively, on someone else, so we must always be letting the light of Christ within us shine out for the world to see (Matthew 5:14-16). It has to be as much a part of our lives as breathing in and out.

What happens when we shine that light, however, depends on the person who sees it. Sometimes we will shine the light and no one will notice. Sometimes we will shine and no one will care. Sometimes we will shine and those who bother to look will be disgusted and shun us. But then there are also those rare moments when someone is looking, seeking, praying, and hoping to find help. In those moments, we will be shinning, and those who are seeking will find the light of Christ within us and, through us, they will find the way to Jesus.

This chapter is entitled "how do I be a disciple" because that's a question that may not be asked very often, in so many words, but it is a question many new converts are confronted with soon after they are baptized. It's not always the case, but it frequently happens that a person who is baptized is someone that is taught a lot about what to do to become a Christian and not as much about what to do **as** a Christian.

You might hear the basic things like "study your Bible" and "pray" and "go to worship on Sundays and Bible class on Wednesday." I'm not going to tell you any of those things are bad. On the contrary, all of those things are essential. They also represent the bare minimum.

Imagine living your physical life only doing the bare minimum; what would that look like? Imagine a person who wakes up in the morning and eats just enough to survive before going back to bed, a person who works their muscles just enough to avoid atrophy, and who shuns basically all social contact with other people. That person is technically alive, but he's hardly living. The quality of his life is also so poor he will not live long and he will certainly not live happily. In fact, people who do begin to act like that are quickly given attention by loved ones, because it's a clear sign of depression.

Many brethren are spiritually depressed and they do not even realize it, because the condition affects the soul instead of the body. Spiritually, they are doing only the bare minimum needed to survive, not realizing that the bare minimum means they are slowly dying, spiritually.

There is so much more to being a Christian than just reading the Bible, praying, and attending a congregational service twice a week. If those things represent the foundation of a proper and healthy spiritual life, then what is

WHAT NEXT?

to be built on that foundation? What is it that goes into this "life" of Christianity? If obeying the Gospel means putting the old self to death and rising to be a new self (Romans 6), then what does that new self...do? You've obeyed the Gospel; you know how to **become** a disciple of Jesus, but maybe you're wondering how to **be** a disciple.

Fortunately, the New Testament is not silent on the subject. To begin with, you should remember that you **are** a disciple. Whether you've been a Christian for five minutes, five years, or five decades, you are not the Master. You are the student of the Master.

Depending on whether or not you love(d) being in school, the prospect of being a student for the rest of your natural life might be a nice thought or a major turn-off. I was terrible in school and rarely made good grades, so it is with great relief that I hear the words of Jesus, regarding what kind of a schooling He gives His disciples...

> "Come unto Me all you that labor and are heavy-laden, and I will give you rest. Take my yoke upon you and learn of Me, for I am meek and lowly in heart, and you shall find rest unto your souls. For My yoke is easy and My burden is light" (Matthew 11:28-30).

MATTHEW L. MARTIN

First of all, notice that Jesus recognizes how hard your old life was. The fact is, a person is always going to be learning lessons in life, either the easy way or the hard way. The Lord's invitation is for people who are weighed down by the heavy load of a hard life to come to Him for help.

What kind of help does He offer? Jesus offers your own kind of schooling. That's what the word "yoke" means in the King James version of this text. It refers to the attachment a student has to a teacher. Back then, general education was not administered the way it is today; a person didn't go to school to learn the basics of history, science, reading, writing, and arithmetic. Instead, you studied under a specialist in some field. You attached (yoked) yourself to a doctor to learn to be a doctor, or a lawyer to learn to be a lawyer, etc.

What kind of yoke does Jesus offer? What kind of schooling does He give to those who want to learn at His feet? Before answering that, we should stop to consider what specialty Jesus has that we want to learn?

If you read the verses earlier in Matthew 11, you see the context of Jesus' great invitation: The Lord was performing great miracles and some from John the Baptist (on behalf of John himself) asked if He really was the Messiah.

WHAT NEXT?

Likewise, many critics of Jesus were quick to attack Him because He did not behave the way they thought the Messiah should. What was the problem: Jesus was acting the way God wanted Him to act. And for that, some doubted and others mocked.

What is the yoke of Jesus? It is the invitation to, like Him, live differently from the rest of the world, to act godly, to love, give, and sacrifice in ways others do not. To be His disciple is to be a student of righteousness, often in the face of persecution, resentment, and ugliness.

What kind of teacher is the Lord? He tells you in the verse: He is "meek and lowly." He is not a teacher that scolds unfairly or disciplines impatiently. He is a teacher that trains and guides His students into living the kind of life He lived.

So here you are, a new Christian. You're now a student of the Messiah. You're expected to learn and grow and live as a disciple. How do you do that? What does that look like? We can open the New Testament and see very clearly what it means to be a disciple.

First, a disciple makes more disciples. Jesus tells us to go into the world and to make disciples of those we meet (Matthew 28:18-20). That means we have to be teachers of the Word, telling others what to do to become Christians as we have done. That can be intimidating and scary for many brethren, especially new brethren, who feel unprepared and inadequate to tell someone about Jesus. I would remind you, however, that you're never going to have all the answers. What you **can** do, however, is tell someone what **you** did to become a child of God.

There's more to it than being a teacher by word; we must also be teachers by example. We have to be living invitations. Through our conduct and character, the people who are looking for a better way to live, and a hope to live for, will find it by seeing how different you are from everyone else who is in the world.

Once again, remember that your Master calls you to be a light in the dark world (Matthew 5:14). You might be the **only** light that someone sees, and if so, that means they will be drawn to you like a moth to a flame. When that happens, you will have the opportunity to make a disciple as the Lord commands.

Something else the Bible teaches us about being a disciple is that we recognize who our true family is. This is where it gets very hard for many followers of Jesus, and for the non-Christian loved ones of Jesus' disciples. You will always have a physical family, and you will always

WHAT NEXT?

love them, care for them, and provide for them however possible. They are yours by blood and that will never change. That being said, you are a Christian now: The old you is dead. You are new. That means you have been raised to a new life and to belong to a new family.

Never is that made more apparent than the occasion recorded in Mark 3, when Jesus sat within the house of one of His disciples and taught many who came to hear Him. As He did, His blood family—His mother Mary and His half-brothers—stood outside, wanting to speak with Him. In response, Jesus looked around the room and said "behold my mother and brothers, for whosoever does the will of God, the same is my mother, brother, and sister" (Mark 3:31-35).

Mary was not His enemy. Jesus was not rejecting Mary or shunning her from His life. In fact, Mary was a follower of Jesus too, being present throughout His ministry. Nevertheless, Jesus took advantage of the teaching opportunity before Him to express to the audience around Him—people that were not blood-relatives—how He viewed them as His followers.

We are not sons and daughters of Mary. We are Gentile people from the other side of the world. And yet, because we do the will of God, the Lord considers us His family. In the case of Mary, that was easy, because Mary was a loyal follower of Jesus. What happens when you become a Christian and your brother does not? What happens when you obey the Gospel and your son refuses? Your blood family is still yours but your entire worldview has now changed: You belong to Christ. Your old life is dead and the new one is His to command (Colossians 3:1-3).

Pray that you are never in a position where you have to choose between a family member and Jesus Christ. Pray also that, should that moment come and you **do** have to choose, that you will choose the Master of eternity over the worldly family you are physically connected to. A disciple of Christ must always put Christ first, and that means recognizing that your true family consists of those who also have put Christ first.

Another thing that defines what it means to be a disciple is the readiness to die. That's a morbid thought that isn't always considered so soon after one is baptized. It ought to be, I think. Throughout history, followers of Jesus have been rejected, threatened, abused and, yes, even killed for their faithfulness.

In some places and in some eras, being killed for following Jesus is rarer than in other times and places, but there are always people who will reject the message you bring them,

WHAT NEXT?

many will reject it forcefully, and some will turn to violence in their rejection. When that happens, death is a possibility. Pretending it isn't does you no good as a disciple.

And while it is perfectly reasonable to look at your life thus far and imagine many more years, filled with many more plans to achieve, children of God diminish the significance of their new life in Christ by worrying about the chance they might die.

As soon as we start worrying about how our faith might get us hurt or killed, we will start censoring ourselves, choosing not to speak when the opportunity arises, choosing not to pursue making someone a disciple as our Master commands.

We cannot be afraid of retribution, even if that means death. Ours should be the attitude of Stephen, who was still proclaiming the Lordship of Jesus even while his enemies were hurling stones against his cranium.

If you want me to tell you **how** to achieve the mindset where you're okay being killed for Jesus, I can't help you there. That's something that has to develop with time and experience. What I can tell you is what James said, which is the more you draw near to Christ, the more He will draw near to you (James 4:8).

MATTHEW L. MARTIN

The longer you are a child of God and the more you live with a sense of total dependency on Jesus, the less the dangers of the world will matter. At least they won't matter enough to stop you from doing what you must. You're probably always going to feel fear when someone puts a gun in your face. The closer you draw to Christ, however, the more content you will be at the possibility that the person with the gun might pull the trigger.

Being a Christian is a life; it's not something you can switch off. Because of that, it's reasonable that, as a new Christian, you might look ahead to the "rest" of your life, for however long that is, and think: "What am I supposed to do now?"

It's really not that complicated. Take the three previous points and summarize them: Remind yourself that you're already dead and raised with Jesus so, naturally, you are prepared to die. With that as your attitude, you will naturally draw close to others who share in that willingness to take up your cross and follow the Lord. Along the way, you will invite others to join you, to take up their crosses, to put their lives to death, and be raised spiritually for Jesus, ready and prepared to die physically for him too.

WHAT NEXT?

After all, what is physical death but an end to the heavy burdens of this world and a comforting rest in the arms of Jesus forever? If the enemy wants to kill us for following God, who are we to stop them? Being executed for faithfulness is basically an express-lane to Jesus. Bring it on, I say.

That being said, while I'm ready for Heaven...I'm not ready **yet**, if you know what I mean. I'm prepared to live for Jesus and die for Him too, but I'm not about to go jumping in front of a bus. The Lord didn't save me so that I **would** be executed for Him. He saved me so that I could be spiritually prepared to be executed for Him should the moment arise.

In the meantime, I intend to live. He saved me so that, before my life here is done, I could be a light in the dark world. That's what it means to be a disciple. It means to reflect the light of Christ, to be set apart, and to shine so that those who are seeking for salvation can find what we found and be saved as we are.

Chapter Six

WHAT DO I DO WITH MY OLD LIFE?

Becoming a child of God involves a series of commitments. I suppose, in the big picture, there's only one commitment that counts and that's the decision you make to put on Christ and serve Him unendingly. Still, that one decision, if you think back, involved several small occasions where you drew a line in the proverbial sand and declared: "That was then, and this is now."

Maybe you were someone who grew up hearing Gospel sermons. Maybe you never attended a "church service" for the first part of your life. However it began, it doesn't matter:

WHAT NEXT?

Focus on the day when you first believed the Gospel. Even if you didn't completely fathom the ramifications of your newfound faith, you still had the idea—even if only implicitly—that your life would never be the same.

Faith in Jesus compels us to respond with action. It is no coincidence and it is not without reason that those actions a faith-filled person undertakes are often described in the New Testament in terms of mortality.

Jesus tells us to "deny ourselves." The phrase implies we stop putting our own self-interests at the top of our mind. That's a radical idea, since it is almost hardwired into us as people to follow after "self-preservation." Yet, here is Jesus—this new Master to whom we have committed our faith—telling us to shed the instinct of "staying alive at all costs."

What follows that phrase? Jesus tells us to "take up our cross..." Only then, after we have done those two things, can we obey the last command: "...and come follow me" (Mark 8:34). And what does it mean to take up the cross? Consider that, to Jesus, taking up the cross meant trekking up Golgotha's hill and dying for all humanity. What else could it mean but for us to take up our instrument of death and die for Him? Does He mean for us to give up our physical lives? If it comes to that, maybe, but it may not ever come to that. There is a death, however, that we **must** submit to.

Paul writes that Christians are to put to death any and all aspects of our lives that harm our soul's salvation (Colossians 3:5). It can be hard to let go of the sins we spent so much of our life pursuing, but that's why we have to deny ourselves. We must let go of those sins if we want to follow Jesus, which is why Jesus commands us to pick up our cross. And we must not just set them aside for later enjoyment but must, as Paul said, "put them to death."

When we "believe in Jesus," what we are actually doing is making a commitment to put our old lives to death. It's no coincidence, then, that the very next thing that happens, after a person believes the Gospel, is repentance of sin. What is repentance, in that case, but the actual putting to death the sin that separates us from Christ?

Repentance is the denial of self. Repentance is the taking up of the cross. Repentance is the moment when a person says: "I am no longer following my own ways: I have made the decision to follow the ways of Jesus." What follows repentance? What else but baptism (Acts 2:38). It is at the point of baptism when those sins are buried in a watery grave and, while you—the baptized person—went down into the water, it is not the same "you" that rises. In being

WHAT NEXT?

baptized, you have buried your old, sinful life and are now freed from sin (Romans 6:3-7).

Belief in Jesus (carrying with it the recognition of His perfection, our imperfection, and His dying for us)) is the acknowledgment that you are a criminal worthy of death. Repentance is akin to the judge signing the order to execute the criminal (yourself). Baptism is the moment when the execution (and the burial) takes place.

All that adds up to this fact: Becoming a Christian, in a lot of ways, amounts to the deliberate, meticulous, coordinated "death of self."

So what comes next?

Not to keep going back to this one thought over and over, but it's worth mentioning again that, when you are baptized, nothing physically happens. You are the same person (on the outside) that came out of the water as you were when you went in. Other than getting wet, there's no discernable difference, and yet the Bible recognizes you as a completely new person. Peter even calls new Christians "newborn babies" (1 Peter 2:2).

To the world, however, you're not new. To the world, you're sixteen years old, or twenty-five, or fifty. Jesus sees you as a brand new person; the rest of the world sees you the same as ever.

MATTHEW L. MARTIN

You've lived a life, made friends, developed habits and interests, formed opinions and, worst of all, shared those opinions all over social media.

Your sins are washed away. Your past mistakes have been forgiven, and they will never be held against you again in the court of God, but I can pull up your Twitter account and start scrolling through your post history. What you said is still there, and it's just asking for someone to come along and scrutinize it, especially once you start talking and acting differently from how you used to.

You changed when you became a Christian. It might not be apparent on the outside, but you know it happened. Everyone around you stayed the same, however, and soon, they're going to start wondering why you're not acting like you used to.

The Apostle Peter alludes to this in his first letter, writing about Christians who used to live all manner of sinful lives. Then, when they obeyed the Gospel, they changed and started acting like Jesus. As a result, their old sinful friends "thought it strange." They wondered why these new Christians did not "run with them" anymore. Eventually, those sinners began to speak evil of the one who used to be their friend, all because they no longer lived how they used to live (1 Peter 4:4).

WHAT NEXT?

While Peter talked about it, the Apostle Paul actually lived it. Saul of Tarsus was a persecutor-extraordinaire, but then he met Jesus, believed in Jesus, repented of his sins, and was baptized into Christ. What happened next? Those same Jews who once sided with him turned against him and even plotted to murder him: Paul's new family in Christ had to sneak him away in a basket lest the mob pounce and kill him (Acts 9:23-25).

How ironic: The one who came to Damascus to oversee the death of Christians ended up leaving Damascus as a Christian being hunted to death. What changed? Not the Jews around Paul; they stayed consistent. What changed was Paul himself. His old life was forgiven by God, but it wasn't forgotten by the world, and that old life dogged him for the rest of his days.

Sometimes, a Christian's old life can be an albatross holding him down. Sometimes it can be a glowing beacon reminding you or others about your shameful past. In a lot of ways, you will never fully be able to escape it. It can be forgiven, but it can hardly be forgotten. So what can you do? You're a Christian now; you've started a new life. What are you supposed to do with your old one?

First, I would invite you to accept the facts previously stated. You can't change the past. You will always "have been" a sinner. You also can't change what others think about your past. If some cynical person refuses to accept that you've changed for the better, that's on them, and you can't control what they think about your past. All you can control is what you do going forward.

In that case, when it comes to your old life, I have two simple pieces of advice. First, your old life is dead: Leave it dead. You killed the old self. You crucified it. Leave it dead. Don't slip back into old habits. Don't fall back into old ways. Live a life that is so totally and obviously different from the one you lived before you obeyed the Gospel that people will **have** to acknowledge you've changed (and for the better).

Yes, you will stumble. You will sin again. Now that you're a Christian, especially as a newborn in Christ, the Devil will set his sights squarely on you, and bring every temptation he can to you, in the hopes of luring you away from Christ. The first few weeks and months of your Christianity can be a particular challenge, because it is in those early days when you start to form new habits. It's in those early days when you start to fit into a new culture, different from the one you previously knew. You can be sure

WHAT NEXT?

the Devil will be trying his best to pull you back into old, familiar, sinful habits.

Christians are not a people immune to sin. We are just as susceptible to the spiritual infection as anyone else. The difference is we carry the antidote with us. When we walk in the light then the blood of Jesus cleanses us from all our sins (1 John 1:7). The Devil won't settle for getting us to slip up here and there; he wants us going back to our old life. He wants us to return to the mud and cover ourselves once more in filth, knowing that if we do, and if we do not repent again, we will be condemned all over again (2 Peter 2:20-22). Resist the urge to live that old life again.

Your old self is dead: Leave it dead.

Second, your old self is buried: Leave it buried. Remember that you became a Christian because you wanted your life to be changed for the better, and you recognized you were powerless to improve it on your own. Jesus offered you something better, on the condition that you "deny self, take up your cross, and follow" Him. The only way you became a child of God was by letting go of your need to run your own life. Instead, you have given your life to Christ, like a sheep that trusts a shepherd.

MATTHEW L. MARTIN

In that respect, a sinner is someone determined to control their own destiny and do things their own way. Unfortunately, all have sinned (Romans 3:23), which means, if left to our own devices, all are destined for Hell. If I try to control my own destiny, I will drive myself into the ditch every single time.

When it comes to my old life, the one I lived with for so long, and the one the world made me feel so comfortable living, the temptation may be to pick and choose when I act like Jesus and when I act like the world. It's easy to look and sound like a Christian on Sunday morning, when I'm sitting with my brethren.

What about the rest of the week? How easy is it to be a Christian at school on Monday morning, or at work on Tuesday afternoon, or at a party on Saturday night? There may be times when I try to take back the control of my life and drive the proverbial car once more, but by doing that, I'm sending a signal, not only to those around me, not only to my Lord, but to myself, that I see Christianity as a part-time lifestyle, and perhaps even as a part-time burden.

You became a Christian by choice. You wanted the Lord to save you not just because you didn't want to go to Hell but because you wanted to go to Heaven. You wanted a better end. Never forget that.

WHAT NEXT?

When you obeyed the Gospel your life changed for the better. So ask yourself: If you had to choose one or the other, would you rather dig up the corpse of your old, condemned, spiritual life, and live like the world for a few decades more, only to be exiled to Hell forever, or would you rather keep your old self buried and press on with Christ, despite the short-term hardships that may come, knowing that the end was eternal bliss with Jesus?

Your old life will always be around, in one form or another. The Lord may "remember your sins no more" but you can bet the Devil will work to make sure you never forget it. You can either let him win and go back to the old, or you can stay "new" (2 Corinthians 5:17) and live the best life from here to eternity.

The world may attack you for it. Your old associates may hate you for it. You may even be called a hypocrite for it. It's a lie: You're not a hypocrite. A hypocrite is someone who tells others not to do a bad thing while they actively engage in doing that bad thing. That's not you. You're someone who used to do bad things, stopped because of a better way, and now invites others to stop and enjoy the blessings you currently experience. That doesn't make you a hypocrite...It makes you an evangelist!

Chapter Seven

WHEN SHOULD I CUT OUT BAD INFLUENCES?

Earlier in this book the point was made that, while you—the new Christian—are a changed person, the fact is, the people around you are not. The people with whom you previously shared common interests, morals, and goals for life, are now a people from whom you have one very stark difference: You are saved and they are not. You are a Christian and they are not. You have put your old life to death and they are still living that same sort of life without a care in the world.

Almost certainly, a new Christian's first response to this would be to sit down and try to convert those friends to Christ. After all, you heard and obeyed the Gospel, so it should be as easy as telling someone else everything you heard and they will obey too. It's that easy right?

No.

The fact is, a number of circumstances that led to your conversion are not duplicatable. That doesn't mean your friends can't be reached; it just means the fact that you were reached does not make it a foregone conclusion that they will be just as receptive. You and your friends—even your family—are similar, and lived within the same sphere of culture and morality, but you're not a hive mind. Each person has his or her own unique life experiences, and the way everyone responds to the reality of sin and the prospect of salvation is unique to each.

While some might wholeheartedly take to heart the notion of the one church, the necessity of baptism, and the unbending truth of the Gospel, others might balk at it all. They might push back on the idea that so many others, who have not obeyed the Gospel, are "lost" and "wrong."

You accepted the truth, and thank God for it, but you accepted it because you wanted to accept it. While you technically had a choice, the decision was so obvious you realized you couldn't, in all good conscience, choose not to obey. It might shock you, as you begin talking to others about Jesus, how rare it is for someone to reach that same conclusion.

As sad as it is to think about, the terrible fact is, many people would rather go to Hell if it meant not having to own up to the reality that they are in the wrong. Likewise, many would rather go to Hell because they realize that, by accepting the Gospel as true, they are admitting that their loved ones, who never obeyed it, are condemned.

There are several reasons why the Lord describes His followers as a minority group (Matthew 7:14). Of all the people that will ever live only a "few" will ever find salvation. One reason is the fact that only a few have a soft enough heart and an open enough mind to accept the truth of Jesus' teaching.

Necessarily, we are surrounded by lost people and, being social creatures, we are surrounded by people we love. When you put those two ideas together, you're left with a bitter truth: We are surrounded by people we love who are lost. And no matter how much we may want to reach them, the odds are "few" of them will ever be saved.

So what do we do? Do we obey the Gospel and immediately start shunning everyone who is not a Christian? How does that square

WHAT NEXT?

with our Master, who went out of his way to talk to, sit beside, and share meals with sinners and outcasted people in society?

No, the solution is not to become monks who live in caves, cut off from society. Likewise, the solution is not to associate exclusively with like-minded brethren, shunning all contact with the lost. We are called to be evangelistic and to make disciples (Matthew 28:19).

At the same time, we are warned about letting the sinful world influence us and draw us away from our Christian calling: Paul specifically reminds us how evil associates corrupt good habits (1 Corinthians 15:33). Jesus said His people needed to be willing to sacrifice whatever was necessary to be saved (Matthew 18:9).

So we must associate with sinners, but not let them corrupt us. We must serve and live amongst sinners, but also be prepared to sacrifice those relationships as needed. It sounds like walking a tightrope, and it naturally leads to the question of the chapter. We know there **are** bad influences. We know we must cut them out. The question is: When do we do that?

Unfortunately, this is not a question that has a simple, plug-and-play sort of answer that you can easily apply to every situation. We're talking about relationships and those are very nebulous things. My advice, therefore, is general. In the end, you're going to have to trust your Bible-trained conscience and, of equal importance, you're going to have to be willing to make the hard choice, to walk away from an influence when you realize it is a bad one.

First of all, you should walk away when the influence **becomes** bad. In other words, as said, when you become a Christian, you don't immediately have to cut out every person you ever associated with before you obeyed the Gospel. But, situationally, you're going to encounter more than a few things—pretty early on—that will make you say "I can't do that" or "I can't go there" or "I gave that up."

When you became a Christian, by virtue of your repentance, you already "cut out" and "walked away from" several bad things. Cutting out the influence of those things should be the natural byproduct of your repentance. If a person decides to cut sugar out of his diet, he doesn't hang out at a bakery all day. One naturally leads to the other.

That said, you can cut out sugar and still be friends with the guy who works at the bakery. Is the guy at the bakery trying to sell you sugar all the time, even when you've made it clear you've given it up? If not, then he is not a bad influence. If he is, then you already know what you have to do; now it's just a matter of having the conviction to do it.

Second, you should walk away when the bad influence becomes effective. In other words, while you're friends with the baker, you might find that just being around him reminds you too much of your old sugar-filled life, leading to a temptation to indulge. The Bible is explicit that we should resist temptation (James 4:7) and pray to avoid being tempted (Matthew 6:13). It's hard to do that when you're choosing to frequent the bakery of sin.

If you're able to be around drunkards without being tempted to drink, then so be it. If you're able to be around people who curse without being tempted to curse, then so be it. The danger comes when we are not only around sinners but doing as sinners do **because** we are around sinners. That leads to Christians living a double life, acting one way with one kind of people and another way with another kind of people. That's hypocrisy, and it damns the soul.

What often happens is a Christian will hang out with sinners and start acting like sinners, but will justify it by saying "I'm reaching them." Don't try to cast yourself as a quasi-Jesus, going in among the sinners of society if, in fact, unlike Jesus, you're not even trying to evangelize to them. If all you're doing is going to Rome and doing as the Romans do, then it's you being influenced, not them. You're not offering them a better way; they're offering you a worse way and you're taking it. You're not reaching them; they're reaching you.

Third, you should walk away when you **do** try to evangelize and they consistently refuse to listen. This is a hard one because it's not about being tempted, per se. In this case, the influencer is not trying to get you to indulge in a sin, but rather is just a person you're trying to get to submit to Jesus, and they just don't want to hear it. What do you do? If it's some random person you met for five minutes at an airport, it might be easy to say "well, I tried..." and walk away. If it's your mother, it's a lot harder to kick the dust off your shoes (Matthew 10:14).

Nevertheless, at some point, you must be prepared to accept that the person you tried to evangelize simply doesn't want the Good News, no matter who that person may be. The Master warns us about "casting pearls before swine" (Matthew 7:6), a curious figure of speech that means exactly what it sounds like: We must not waste our time on someone that does not consider the Message of any value.

WHAT NEXT?

You might wonder: What's the harm? This person isn't trying to lead you into wickedness. They're just a lost person that stubbornly refuses to obey the Gospel. Where's the danger in talking to them about it over and over? As said, these things are not precise; you just have to get a feeling for when it has become a problem.

The problem, in this case, comes when you're spending all your energy on someone who doesn't care, when that same energy could be better spent trying to find someone who does. If you don't think the Devil will use your heart, your relationships, and your love for the people close to you against you, then you have greatly underestimated the depths of his depravity.

The time **will** come when you will have to walk away from one for whom your love has influenced you out of effective evangelism; I just hope your conviction and love for Christ is strong enough to make the hard choice to walk away.

Finally, you should walk away when Christ becomes secondary, or when the world starts to take precedence over your Christian family. In other words, when the influencer in question is asking you to put his needs above the demands of God, that's the moment when you have to choose, all over again, between Jesus and the world.

MATTHEW L. MARTIN

When the Apostle Paul wrote to the Colossians about the Lord, he does not refer to Him as "the most important part of our lives." Instead, Paul refers to Jesus simply as "our life" (Colossians 3:4). Jesus is not a part of our life; He's not even the most important part of our lives. Jesus **is** our life. He is everything, and everything we do has to be done through the prism of our Christianity, as Paul later says in that same context (Colossians 3:17).

Jesus Himself said that a person who desired to follow Him must be willing to forsake anything and everything necessary, whether that is our spouse, our sibling, our parent, or our livelihood (Matthew 19:29). Does that mean I **have** to forsake everything? No. I don't have to forsake cherry Dr. Pepper. But if, in some bizarre circumstance, I had to choose between the two, I would choose my Lord. Whatever the choice is, if Jesus is on the one side, it doesn't matter what is on the other; I'm choosing Jesus.

I am dead and my life is hid with Christ in God (Colossians 3:3). Christ was regularly around sinners, the way a candle's light is regularly in a dark room. Christ's light was never smothered by the darkness; His light repelled the darkness. Any influence that draws me away from my life in the light of Christ, and any influencer that asks me to give preference to something dark that

WHAT NEXT?

diminishes the light of my Christianity, and smothers me again in darkness, is something I must be prepared, not only to **walk** away from, but to **run** away from with great haste.

Again, knowing when and how to identify a bad influence is a difficult task, but it is one that grows easier as you mature in the faith. The longer you live as a Christian, and the more you replace your old sinful habits with new spiritual ones, the more the darkness of the world stands out. In that case, it will be easier—with a Bible-trained conscience—to know when you're influencing something for the better, as opposed to when you're being influenced for the worse.

Often, though, walking away from a bad influence means making a hard choice. Remember, you have already obeyed the Gospel. You have already made a hard choice: You faced the facts about yourself, and you made the decision to give up your old life. You did it then; if push comes to shove, are you prepared to do it again, and again, and as many times as the Devil will try to draw you back? I think you are because that's the calling. That's the narrow way we walk.

And few there be that find it.

Chapter Eight

WHAT IF I SIN?

There's no need to hide the fact that we obeyed the Gospel because we didn't want to go to Hell. Yes, it's true that we also wanted a life with Christ, both now and forever, but it's also the case that the prospect of a life perpetually separated from God is terrifying.

Human nature—given to us by God— inclines us toward self-preservation, something that does not go away when we obey the Gospel, despite Jesus telling us to "deny self." Instead, our instinct for self-preservation is refocused to a spiritual level: Christians are okay with dying, but the idea of dying lost—spiritually dead—is something we will fight tooth and nail to avoid.

WHAT NEXT?

And yet we are regularly tempted to sin and often find ourselves indulging in activities that not only condemn the soul but which we turned away from and were baptized to wash away. Why do we do this? The simple reason is because our instinct for **spiritual** self-preservation has to be trained, fine-tuned, and developed over the years.

There's a reason brethren who have been faithful Christians for fifty years seemingly have an easier time living faithfully than someone who has only been a Christian for a year or so: The longer you live with Jesus, the easier it is to be repulsed by the Devil's temptations.

In the meantime, new Christians won't often have the same feeling about indulging in a sin as they would if they were standing in front of an open door in an airplane, wondering about jumping without a parachute. In the latter case, our natural desire to stay alive keeps our feet in the plane. In the former case, Christians eat the forbidden fruit without regard for their spiritual life. Why? Because they haven't taught themselves (and haven't yet allowed the Word of God to teach them) the importance of spiritual self-preservation.

Until that feeling develops, new Christians are going to struggle with temptation and sin. The Devil isn't going to give you a happy honeymoon with Jesus, after all. This is the time when you are the most vulnerable and, like the predatory lion he is (1 Peter 5:8), he will strike when you are at your weakest. That raises the important question of the chapter: What do I do when I sin?

To begin, let's address two related questions that are sure to come up in a topic like this. First of all: Can we sin? Is it even possible for children of God to sin? Someone who might argue you can not is likely to use what John wrote to justify their position: "Whosoever is born of God doth not commit sin; for his seed remaineth in him: and he cannot sin, because he is born of God (1 John 3:9).

However, is John using the word "cannot" to mean an action is impossible or one that is impermissible. I'm reminded of what John himself said when ordered by his government to stop preaching Jesus: "we cannot but speak the things which we have seen and heard (Acts 4:20)." Does that mean John was unable to be silent or does it mean he was commanded to speak and thus was obligated to obey? It's the latter and I thnk we all understands that.

In the same book wherein John says that Christians "cannot sin" (1 John 3:9), John also writes that if we say we have no sin we deceive

WHAT NEXT?

ourselves (1 John 1:8), and that we must confess our sins (1 John 1:9). Can Christians sin? Yes, the ability to disobey God on Thursday is not taken away from you just because you obeyed the Gospel on Wednesday. You still have free will. You're not permitted to sin, by commandment, but you still retain the ability to do so, if you choose to disobey that commandment.

There once was a man named Simon. He was a con man and a trickster, who deceived many of Samaria into thinking he had Divine power. After hearing the Gospel preached by the evangelist Philip, Simon believed and was baptized (Acts 8:9-13). Later, after witnessing actual Divine power, as performed by Peter and John, Simon tried to bribe the Apostles into giving him the power they could do. This was a sin, and Peter called him out on it, demanding that he repent of his wickedness (Acts 8:18-22). Simon was a Christian and Simon sinned. He wasn't supposed to, but he was weak, he was tempted, and he gave in.

The other related question is this: Even if Christians **can** sin (we can, but we shouldn't), will it even condemn us if we do? In other words, once I'm saved, am I not "always" saved? On that point, we return to the previous answer: Why would Peter command Simon to repent if he was in no danger of condemnation? Why would any of us live and suffer for the cause of Christ if, after we obeyed the Gospel, we could just run and hide and deny the faith whenever it was convenient, without any fear of repercussion from the Divine Judge?

Furthermore, if my obeying the Gospel means I am saved no matter how sinful I act afterward then, really, I am the master and God is my servant. He must save me no matter how offensive I am to His holiness through my sinfulness. I can curse His name from now to the end of my life and, in the end, He cannot send me to Hell. He is unable. I have Him on a leash and I am leading Him around.

That's not reality.

In reality, a Christian can fall away (Hebrews 6:6). A Christian can fall from Grace (Galatians 5:4). A Christian can return to the filth of sin and make their spiritual end worse than if they had never obeyed the Gospel in the first place (2 Peter 2:20-22). Those verses are undeniable, but perhaps the starkest, most chilling text with regards to this topic comes from a parable Jesus taught (Matthew 18:23-35)...

The Lord once told a story of a servant who owed his master a great debt and could not pay. In mercy, the master forgave the debt

WHAT NEXT?

entirely. Later, that forgiven servant went to one of his fellow servants, who owed him a small debt, and demanded that he pay him in full.

The hypocrisy so enraged the master that he literally revoked the forgiveness of the servant's great debt and ordered him to be delivered to the tormenters till the whole debt was paid off. The very debt that the master said was forgiven was, because of the servant's evil actions, "unforgiven." In conclusion, Jesus says that is exactly what the Heavenly Father will do to us if we—a forgiven people—do not forgive others who ask it of us.

Yes, we are still able to sin. Yes, doing so will still condemn us as it would before we were baptized. In light of those two realities, someone may ask: What then is the point of being saved? If I'm just as in danger of condemnation now as I was then, what does it matter if I am saved?

To ask the question is to answer it: It matters because you are saved! It matters because, just as you chose to become a Christian, you can choose to stay faithful, too. You don't have to condemn yourself. That's the wonderful thing about the Gospel. Before Jesus came, we all were condemned because we all had sinned (Romans 3:23). Now, thanks to Christ, we all have the freedom to be forgiven of our sins, and not just the sins we committed in the past, but those we will commit after we are saved, too. The same blood of Christ that washed our old sins away (Acts 22:16) washes our new sins away, as well (1 John 1:7).

So how do we bridge the gap between the truth that I can still be condemned after I am saved and the truth that my sins can regularly be washed away after I sin? To that, John provides the answer: "But if we walk in the light, as He is in the light, we have fellowship one with Another, and the blood of Jesus Christ His Son cleanseth us from all sin (1 John 1:7)."

In order for us to be cleansed of our sins we must walk in the light of Christ. If we get out of that light (and we are free to get out of it, as we've already noted—2 Peter 2:20-22) then we lose access to the sin-cleansing power of the blood. If we stay out of the light, then we return to condemnation.

Here's the great news: If we stay in the light then not only are our past sins washed, but our sins are "continually washed." As long as we're in the light we exist in a perpetually saved state. If you add 2 and 2 you will always get 4. If you add 2 and 1 you will never get 4. If you walk in the light you will always be saved. If you don't walk in the light you will never be saved.

The thing is, though, walking in the light is a messy process. Imagine the way to Heaven as a

WHAT NEXT?

straight line from here to there: The only Person who ever made the journey from here to there in a straight, unwavering line was Jesus Himself. For the rest of us, our line looks like this...

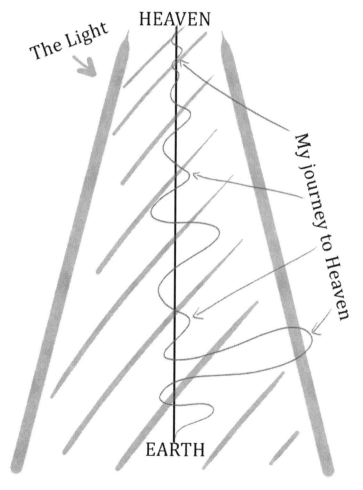

You'll notice how un-straight it is. There is a point, early in the journey, when I went so far away that I got out of the light. I repented and turned back, however, and then continued on my way. You'll also notice that the longer I went on the journey, the more like Jesus I acted, and the deviations grew less pronounced.

Hopefully, no one who obeys the Gospel comes out of the water thinking they are now expected to be perfect or lose their salvation forever. That is just one of many misconceptions people have regarding the issue of Christians' sinning. You aren't given liberty to sin, don't misunderstand, but you are given grace to cover you when you **do** sin. That's the big difference.

You are placed in the light of Christ and asked to be faithful (Revelation 2:10). You're not going to be perfect, but being faithful doesn't mean being perfect; it means repenting and turning back when you aren't. When you look at the chart on the previous page, you can see the time when I veered out of the light; that was a time when I sinned and did not repent. Eventually, I came to my senses and turned back to Christ and, when I did, I went back into the saving light once more.

There are many more misconceptions when it comes to the issue of Christians' sinning. Another can be found in the title of this chapter,

WHAT NEXT?

"what **if** I sin." The use of the word "if" is sure to rile up someone who forgot what the Apostle John wrote: "My little children, these things write I unto you, that ye sin not. **And if any man sin**, we have an advocate with the Father, Jesus Christ the righteous (1 John 2:1)."

First, John repeats the commandment: "Do not sin." Then, he recognizes the futility in obeying that commandment without ever slipping up: "**If** you sin you have an advocate..."

The word "if" here doesn't imply a condition, because the condition of sin is one which we will all encounter. Instead, the word implies a hypothetical, because while it is certain you will sin, you're still commanded not to. Changing the title to "when I sin" ignores the fact that I'm not supposed to sin. Rightly is it phrased as an "if" proposition, because I shouldn't be sinning. So, in the hypothetical scenario wherein I **do** sin, what then?

What does John say? Look at the rest of the text in question: "My little children, these things write I unto you, that ye sin not. And if any man sin, we have an advocate with the Father, Jesus Christ the righteous: And he is the propitiation for our sins: and not for ours only, but also for the sins of the whole world. And hereby we do know that we know him, if we keep his commandments (1 John 2:1-3)."

MATTHEW L. MARTIN

What if you sin? You repent and start keeping His commandments again, that's what. After all, what is sin? Sin is breaking God's commandments (1 John 3:4). To repent is to change the mindset from worldliness to Godliness. Put those two ideas together, and you have John's advice here: if you sin (and stop obeying God's commands) then repent (and start obeying them again).

Another misconception people have is the belief that God is hovering over us like a person with a fly swatter, ready to strike the first time we slip up. If you want to know what the character of God is, you only need to look at the Lord Jesus during His ministry. How many times did the Lord show patience with His disciples (especially Peter)? Did He rebuke them? Yes. Did He correct them? Yes. Did He kick them out of His sphere of fellowship every time they messed up? No. Why not? Because whenever they messed up, they did not quit following Him. They learned better, and started doing better as a result.

The lesson to learn from the Ministry of Jesus is this: If you mess up, then repent, keep following Jesus, and you will be fine. Your place in Jesus' Kingdom is not so tenuous that you are in and out, in and out, in and out, every time you mess up. Your journey to Heaven will be a

WHAT NEXT?

wobbly one, but it will still be a journey to Heaven.

Another misconception is the idea that we can't help but be sinners, so there's no incentive to try and resist the temptation to sin. If you've ever seen someone shrug and say "well we're all sinners" when talking about brethren, that is the genesis of this misconception. If we're all just sinners anyway then righteousness is hopeless. Why bother?

We are not sinners.

Christians are not sinners; we are saints. Do Christians sin? Yes, but sinners are not saints and saints are not sinners. Do not be ashamed to refer to yourself as a saint. Jesus paid too high a price to purchase your soul and make you a saint only for you to run from that title and call yourself a sinner. Listen to Paul:

> *"Be ye therefore followers of God, as dear children; And walk in love, as Christ also hath loved us, and hath given himself for us an offering and a sacrifice to God for a sweetsmelling savour. But fornication, and all uncleanness, or covetousness, let it not be once named among you, as becometh saints" (Ephesians 5:1-3).*

MATTHEW L. MARTIN

The Apostle says very clearly that you are a follower of God and a child of God. You are someone who walks in love and avoids sin. Why? Because sinful things are not becoming of saints. Listen to Paul: Stop calling yourself a sinner. You're not a sinner. You've been set apart from sin: You're a saint (that's what the word means: "set apart").

Even when you mess up and sin, you're still not a "sinner" by name, because you have gotten out of the lifestyle. Now you're in the sanctified lifestyle. You used to be someone who sinned because it was your way of life; now righteousness is your way of life and sin is the exception that you regret and repent of as soon as it happens.

The only thing that can condemn your soul is you, but thanks be to the Lord that He has given you the power to become a child of God (John 1:12). Like all children, we will try to imitate our Father, and though we will not do it perfectly, we will at least try to do our best...or maybe we'll try to try to do our best. That's probably more accurate.

Never forget the mercy of God exists. The same mercy that saved you from your sins is still saving you today, as long as you are faithful. And if you ever stop, never forget the mercy of God still exists. The same mercy that offered your salvation the first time offers you restoration if you sin again. All you have to do is repent and turn back.

Do you remember reading the account of Peter walking on the water (Mark 14:22-32)? It's one of the more well-known moments in Jesus' ministry. The Apostles were on a boat when a storm began to rage around them. Panicked and fearful for their lives, the disciples looked onto the water and saw the Lord walking toward them, unbothered by the storm that had them so frightened.

Excited, Peter asked the Lord for permission to join Him and, amazingly, the Lord invited him onto the water. Without a second's hesitation, Peter jumped off the boat and walked on the water toward his lord.

You know what happened next.

Peter took his eyes off Jesus and "began to sink" (Mark 14:30). The same miraculous power that allowed the disciple to stand on water was now slowly letting that water overtake him. Peter didn't drop like a rock the way a, well, a **rock**, would do if you threw it into a pond. Instead, he slowly started to descend into the watery depths. Fortunately, Peter had the good sense to reach out his hand and take hold of his Master.

Peter shouldn't have taken his eyes off Jesus. We shouldn't either. If we do, we can remember the example of Peter: If we only reach out and take the hand of Jesus, all will be right again.

Do you know what else is amazing? Even though Peter messed up by taking his eyes off Jesus, Mark says that when Jesus picked His disciple up out of the water, they both walked back to the ship (Mark 14:32). In other words, Peter walked on water again, even after he messed up the first time. To answer the question of the chapter: If you sin, reach out for Jesus.

He's waiting to receive you again.

WHAT NEXT?

MATTHEW L. MARTIN

Chapter Nine

HOW DO I DEAL WITH DOUBT?

Very likely, about five seconds before you were dipped into the waters of your baptism, someone asked you "do you believe that Jesus Christ is the Son of God?" To that, you said "I do." Maybe, instead of being asked, you were given the opportunity to speak, in which case you said something like: "I believe Jesus Christ is the Son of God."

That's how it usually goes before someone is baptized into Christ: They stand in the water and they confess the faith they already had: You believe Jesus Christ is the Son of God. That belief is an extension of your belief in God's existence. After all, if you know that Jesus is God's "Son,"

WHAT NEXT?

then you must also know there is a "Father" in Heaven.

So, you believe. Of course you do: Why else would you be baptized? You wouldn't submit to such a strange and seemingly arbitrary command unless you had good reason to do so, and what better reason is there than "because God told me to."

Or would you?

Maybe you were only baptized because your parents were pressuring you. Maybe they weren't pressuring you directly, but perhaps you felt pressured because you knew they were expecting it, praying for it, wondering about it, etc. Maybe many of your peers were being baptized and, being around their age, you thought you might look out of place if you didn't do as they did.

Maybe you were caught up in the moment after an emotional sermon; perhaps several others responded and you just got swept up in the emotion of it all and walked down the aisle the same way many others did.

Or maybe you genuinely decided that you needed to do it. No one else told you, pressured you, or even lovingly encouraged you. On your own, you realized what you had to do, and you did it. Why? Because you read your Bible and you believed what God commanded.

And now—be it a day later, a week later, maybe even ten years later—you find yourself asking the question, not to others, but internally: "Is all this even real? Does any of this even matter? Is it even true?"

You have doubts, and because of the nature of these doubts, you're probably terrified to vocalize them. So many people around you are living (seemingly) happy, Christian lives. They all seem supremely confident in what they believe. You don't hear them expressing doubts about things as fundamental as the existence of God or the authority of the Bible. You think you're on an island, being the only Christian around who sometimes wonders if everything you believe is true or just a well-intentioned fairy tale.

Guess what? You're not alone in thinking that. Furthermore, there is nothing wrong with questioning and wondering. The only way such thoughts become sinful is when a person refuses to listen, or stubbornly holds onto their doubts in the face of evidence to the contrary.

God is not so insecure that He doesn't want you questioning His existence. By all means, question it. God knows that every time an honest person looks for Him, they will find Him. He's not worried that someone will "discover the

WHAT NEXT?

truth" that He doesn't exist. He knows He exists! Unfortunately, there is no Scripture in the Bible that mentions someone specifically searching for whether or not God exists.

Back then, the idea of challenging the notion of God's existence was unheard of. The debate back then was about **which** "god" was more powerful, yours or mine, etc. Nevertheless, God regularly invited His people—in those times when they chose to forget He was out there—to look for Him and find Him.

> *I am the LORD, and there is none else, there is no God beside me: I girded thee, though thou hast not known me: That they may know from the rising of the sun, and from the west, that there is none beside me. I am the LORD, and there is none else (Isaiah 45:5-6).*

The nation of Judah had stopped listening to God. They had cut God out of their lives and were trusting in themselves to get through their problems. In that case, there's no difference between them and atheists who deny the existence of God. Judah might not have denied God's existence, but by ignoring Him, they might as well have.

What does God say to that? He points out that He is everywhere: From the rising of the sun in the East to the setting of the sun in the West. From one side to the next, God is there and none can compare. If you look for Him, you will find Him.

So why do we doubt?

For one thing, we live in a world that casually dismisses the idea of God. The culture of the world today is one that, much like Judah of old, tries its best to pretend there is no God watching us, no God listening to us, and no God who will judge us at the last day.

And how convenient is that? Without a God above us, we are free to forge our own path, write our own destiny, and do whatever feels right to us. Moral anarchy reigns: Without an absolute standard of right and wrong there **is** no right or wrong; everything is either good or bad "to me" regardless of whether it is good or bad "to you."

That's the current environment, especially in the United States and Europe. Keep in mind, the idea that there is no God did not **lead** people to conclude we can do whatever we want. Instead, the desire to do whatever we wanted led people to talk themselves into the belief that

WHAT NEXT?

there is no God. It started with a desire to do evil: To justify evil, humanity "killed" the Judge of all things evil.

"God is dead," Nietzsche said. In fact, Nietzsche went on to say "belief in the Christian God has become unbelievable." To him—the German philosopher of the late-19th Century— our world had evolved beyond the need for a God to regulate morality. Nietzsche specifically said that "morality is an interpretation."

Sure, that was 150 years ago, more or less, but it takes a while for the postulations of a philosopher to seep into the mainstream zeitgeist of society at large. A century after Nietzsche died, the idea that God was a myth and that we are on our own was no longer an idea only accepted by "academics," but was the default position of so-called "civilized society."

Now, to be a believer is to be the exception, not the rule, and to promote atheism is to promote mainstream thinking. On the other hand, to promote faith in God and trust in His word is to invite ridicule. At least, that's how it was when I was younger.

Today, it's even worse. How? Today being a believer rarely even produces ridicule from nonbelievers. Today, notions of faith in Someone greater than ourselves are basically ignored. People who hold to such faith-filled positions have become people to be pitied, whose ideas aren't important enough to be challenged intellectually. "The science is settled," they say.

When I was younger, atheism was evangelized and shouted about loudly by its acolytes. Today, it's accepted as commonly as the fact that the sky is blue. If you choose to say otherwise you will privately be thought a fool, and certainly don't expect anyone to go to bat for you if you state your contarian beliefs out loud. Instead, expect to hear plenty of casual conversation about how God doesn't exist, as though this is an understood fact not worth debating.

I say all that to say this: If you have doubts about God's existence or the Bible's authority, understand that 99% of it is the result of living in a world where you are inundated with talk about how "atheism is normal; faith is abnormal." After a while, it's no wonder that some brethren start to question what they believe. There's only so much bombardment a fortification can take, and the walls of our faith are daily bombarded by atheistic artillery.

A lot of brethren wrestle with doubts simply through osmosis: They live in the world and hear nothing but things which conflict with their understanding of God and the world through the Bible. Children are taught the

WHAT NEXT?

universe is billions of years old at the same time they're taught the sun is 93 million miles away. One of those ideas is an observable, provable scientific fact. The other idea is that the universe is billions of years old.

Good luck, however, getting a first grader to appreciate the difference between those two things, when both are taught by the same well-intentioned science teacher, who probably attends one church or another in town, and who just repeats, without a second thought, the atheistic curriculum she was ordered by the secular government to teach to our children.

You have doubts? I'm not surprised! You've been hearing ungodly nonsense since Kindergarten! The question is: How do we deal with doubts? How do we hold on to the faith we proclaimed in Jesus moments before we were baptized into Him?

First, understand that facts are only half the equation. If what you're looking for is a single bit of information you can digest that will automatically take away every doubt you have about spiritual things, I'm sorry but it doesn't work like that.

That being said, if you wish you had something—like a simple document you could read—that would just tell you "God is real and so is your salvation," then I've got good news for you: The Bible is sitting on your shelf right now just waiting to be read!

Really, the issue of "dealing" with doubt is this: There is no way to turn doubt off. You will probably find yourself worrying less about such things as you continue to study and grow in Christ, only for new doubts to creep in, taking on new forms, as you get older. This is going to be a challenge you live with forever, wondering for a moment or three if you're doing the right thing, if you're doing the right thing the right way, if what you believe is true or not. Those moments may linger or they may pass as soon as they come, but they will always come, here and there, for the rest of your life.

And that's okay. Read the Psalms and you'll find countless examples of people—God's people—expressing frustration with God, crying to God, wondering why God isn't listening to them, doesn't care about them, and won't help them. None of those people ever doubted God's existence, but instead they acknowledged God was out there, and wondered why He didn't care. How is that any better?!

At one point, David cried out, "God why have you forsaken me?!" (Psalm 22:1), only later to admit, "okay, You haven't forsaken me; it just feels like it sometimes" (Psalm 22:24). In other words,

WHAT NEXT?

David started with a frustrated cry, then talked himself through the problem, until he was able to admit what he always knew. And God let him work through that whole process. Again, Jehovah is not so insecure that He needs to forbid you from asking "is God really out there?" He knows He's out there, He knows He has given you the means to find Him; He just needs for you to look and admit you have found Him when you do.

Second, if it's God's existence you doubt, then look around and apply common sense. The world—the whole universe—cries out and insists there is a Creator (Psalm 19:1). The moon is **just** close enough to our planet to stimulate the development of life on earth. Likewise the sun is **just** far enough away that we neither freeze nor burn up. The stars are a marvel to behold, and are uncountable in number (supposedly there are a septillion in the universe, but that is purely a guess). This universe came from somewhere. Those stars came from somewhere.

If the following sentence sounds elementary, then so be it: This universe did not come from nothing. Regardless of whether it is vast or microscopic, a thing which exists did not spontaneously come into being of its own volition. In the words of the inimitable Curtis Cates, past director of the Memphis School of

Preaching: "Nothing" did not just get busy and make "something."

If that is too simplistic for some, too bad. I would argue the modern scientific community knows there is no answer to the question "where did the universe come from" that doesn't involve **something** greater than the universe being the instigator, and so, rather than admit there must have been a so-called "first mover," they obscure their conundrum by talking about everything **but** the origins of things.

In other words, if just saying "something didn't come from nothing" is too simplistic, then whatever scientists today are saying is too convoluted, intentionally.

The simplest explanation is often the correct one: Lesser things do not produce greater things. This universe—vast as it is—exists. Therefore, something even bigger created it. And, based on the particularness of it, that something was an intelligent designer.

Suggest an intelligent child built a LEGO castle and no one bats an eye. Certainly no one would be stupid enough to suggest the bucket of LEGOs just up and built themselves. And yet, suggest that an intelligent God built the universe and everyone loses their mind.

The "Fermi Paradox" is a fascinating little thought experiment. Basically, it asks "If all

WHAT NEXT?

evidence points to there being extra-terrestrial intelligent life within a perceivable distance from us...why haven't we perceived them?"

In other words, according to scientists, the odds that earth is the only planet around that has intelligent life is too improbable to be true. Therefore, there must be another planet out there that is just as intelligent and just as capable of sending satellites and radio waves, etc, into outer space as we are. And, if that's true, then why haven't we found them? Why haven't they communicated with us?

The frustrating thing about the Fermi Paradox is that, while it concedes there must be additional intelligent life out there, it never dares to suggest that a "more" intelligent life could be out there, existing beyond the farthest star, and that He **has** communicated with us. They wonder why comparable aliens haven't talked to us, but laugh when we suggest a great God already has. What's the difference, on an astronomical level, other than scale? And I would argue the "scale" of God is a great case to make for His existence: Who else is big enough to have done all this?

But perhaps it's not God that you doubt, but the Bible. I wonder if some people have the impression that the Bible just fell out of the sky, bound in leather, with little tabs on the side so you can quickly go right to the book you're looking for. It shouldn't take you more than three seconds to think about that before you conclude that's not how it happened.

The Bible as it is today is the product of thousands of years' worth of incremental steps. We went from stone tablets, to papyrus, to incredibly thin paper to, now, having it in digital form on our phones.

Doubts people have about the Bible often stem from a lack of understanding about all the work that went into taking us from the original writings of Moses, David, Isaiah, Luke, Paul, etc, to the copied, translated, and printed pages we use today.

First of all, our Bibles were not just "copied." Atheists who try to discredit the Bible will say it's akin to making a photocopy of a photocopy, over and over, with diminishing returns on the image every time. That's an unfair comparison because the reason a copy of a copy (etc) is degraded compared to the original is due to a limitation in the machinery. If there was a machine that could produce a perfect copy every time then you could produce a perfect copy of a perfect copy every time and never suffer diminishing returns.

And that's the standard the original copyists used with the Bible. They did not just

WHAT NEXT?

"copy" the manuscripts. They meticulously transcribed them, not thought for thought, and not even word for word, but letter for letter, carefully ensuring that each page they copied was identical to the former, which was identical to the original.

Those copies were translated and, while there are some "bad" translations out there (due to modern translators having biases and agendas), the original manuscripts were originally translated by men more akin to scientists than religious scholars, interested in textual preservation and transmission than they were pushing agendas.

You can trust your Bible.

The question is, do you want to? If a person doesn't want obey the Bible, it doesn't matter how accurate the text is. There were people during the days of the Old Testament, for example, who literally heard the voice of God and still didn't obey. They had "no doubt" God was real, but they didn't want to listen, so they didn't. Your Bible is the Word of God; whether or not you obey it is not dependent on proof, but on your **willingness** to obey it.

The Bible was written by inspiration. The Apostle Paul writes that "All scripture is given by inspiration of God, and is profitable for doctrine, for reproof, for correction, for instruction in righteousness: That the man of God may be perfect, throughly furnished unto all good works (2 Timothy 3:16-17)."

The type of inspiration the Bible claims is a (1) Divine, (2) verbal, (3) plenary inspiration. Those three descriptions tell you (1) by whom, (2) in what way, and (3) how much.

It is a work of "plenary" inspiration, meaning the totality of it—not just bits and pieces—is inspired. Shakespeare derived his worldly inspiration for the play "Macbeth" from the real-life Scottish King. But not all of the play came from the King; parts were altered to flatter the current English King James. The Bible, however, contains plenary inspiration: The entirety of it, from Genesis 1 to Revelation 22, is inspired.

It is a work of "verbal" inspiration, meaning that every word is given by God. That doesn't mean it was dictated from God to man, like a boss reciting a letter to a secretary to type up for him. The Bible writers did hear God's voice, but in their own thoughts. God looked at the vocabulary of each person, and best chose the word—their words—that fit what He wanted written. God gave Moses the information about the Creation, and Moses wrote that information from his own thoughts, in his own style, guided into perfect accuracy by God.

WHAT NEXT?

It is "Divine" inspiration, meaning the source of the inspiration was God, not current events or personal opinions. The source was the Father Himself.

King David wrote: "The Spirit of the LORD spake by me, and his word was in my tongue" (2 Samuel 23:2). HIS word was on MY tongue, David said. God's words were filtered through David's language, vocabulary, and even personal history, in order to create something Divinely accurate but unique to the writer.

Jeremiah said: "Then the LORD put forth his hand, and touched my mouth. And the LORD said unto me, Behold, I have put my words in thy mouth (Jeremiah 1:9). The same idea David expressed is here expressed by the prophet, and yet the way Jeremiah wrote was different from the way David wrote. They lived generations apart and had different personalities; naturally their styles would differ, but the writing itself remained inspired.

In the New Testament, you can read the inspired words of someone a thousand years removed from David or Jeremiah; the words sound different, but the content is the same.

The Apostle Paul said: "Now we have received, not the spirit of the world, but the spirit which is of God; that we might know the things that are freely given to us of God. Which things also we speak, not in the words which man's wisdom teacheth, but which the Holy Ghost teacheth; comparing spiritual things with spiritual" (1 Corinthians 2:12-13). Paul said his words came from God.

The Apostle Peter said: "Knowing this first, that no prophecy of the scripture is of any private interpretation. For the prophecy came not in old time by the will of man: but holy men of God spake as they were moved by the Holy Ghost" (2 Peter 2:20-21). In other words, the writers of the Bible didn't get together privately to figure out what to say; they spoke as they were moved by the Holy Spirit.

And I know that is exactly the point atheists will attack: They will say the Bible writers precisely did what Peter says they didn't do: They got together and concocted the lies found in the Bible.

The problem with that is simple: If they were all writing lies, and they all knew they were lies, why were they willing to die for the lies they were telling? No one dies for a lie. You might kill for a lie, you might be killed fighting for a lie, and you might die over a lie that you thought was the truth, but no one has ever willingly sacrificed themselves for something they knew was not true. Our instinct for self-preservation is too strong. And atheists expect me to believe

WHAT NEXT?

that, of all the Apostles who were apparently in on the supposed-conspiracy to fabricate all of Christianity, not only did just one of them die for something they knew was a lie, but that **all** of them died for something they knew was a lie?! You're telling me not one of them said "okay, wait, don't cut off my literal head; we made it all up!"

Think about this: Even if that **had** happened, that still wouldn't be enough to disprove the Bible. It only would prove that one of them was too scared to die and was willing to say whatever his executor wanted to hear. But the fact that not one of them did that, but instead went happily to the chopping block, confident that Jesus was resurrected and His Word was true, absolutely is proof that the Bible is not a lie.

The idea that an atheist would say, with a straight face, that the Apostles "just made all that stuff up" is laughable. That's the real fairy tale, not the Bible.

Having a momentary doubt about spiritual things is understandable. It is a sign that you're facing hard truths and wrestling with them. If anything, it's a sign of growth. The danger only comes when you let doubts fester, when you are afraid to confront them and seek out answers.

When that happens, the casual lies of the world take root in the mind and lead faithful brethren into condemnation.

Doubts do not have to take root. They should be seen as opportunities to examine the truth of God, to consider what is written in the Word of God, and to trust that the Creator of everything will see you through.

God is not dead and His word is not a lie.

WHAT NEXT?

Chapter Ten

WHERE DO I BEGIN AS A BIBLE STUDENT?

Whether bound in leather or digitized on a phone screen, the Word of God must be an ever-present companion to the Christian. We must know the Book. That being said, for many new Christians it can be hard to know where to begin. After all, it's a big book.

I can start on page 1 (Genesis 1:1) and read to page 1,000 (Revelation 22:21) and maybe come away with a few dozen key thoughts and ideas, and never feel like I grasped what God was trying

WHAT NEXT?

to get me to understand. Since being a Bible student is as essential to the life of a Christian as breathing oxygen is to living on earth, this book is going to take the next several chapters exploring that idea in a few different ways, beginning with the question at the top of this chapter: Where do I begin?

On one occasion, a law-scholar asked Jesus the most important question ever to be asked: "What shall I do to inherit eternal life?" Of course, His motivation was not pure-of-heart; Luke tells us he asked the question with a desire to test Jesus (Luke 10:25).

The Lord (no surprise) was ready: He turned the question around and forced the law-man to give the answer. "What is written in the Law? How readest thou?" Jesus asked. Note that Jesus did not ask for the man's commentary on the Law; He asked solely for a reading, to let the Word of God speak for itself (Luke 10:26).

Put on the spot, the man had no choice but to quote the texts he knew so well. He referenced the words of Moses (from Deuteronomy and Leviticus) by saying "Thou shalt love the Lord thy God with all thy heart, and with all thy soul, and with all thy strength, and with all thy mind; and thy neighbour as thyself" (Luke 10:27).

MATTHEW L. MARTIN

Much as I would love to write more about the meaning behind those words, that's not why I referenced that conversation. The point is, the lawyer's quote, to answer Jesus' question, was taken from two different sources. The first half came from Deuteronomy 6, while the end was taken from Leviticus 19. In other words, the Jews did not quote and use Scripture the way most western Bible students do.

First of all, they memorized the Word of God from childhood and thus, by adulthood, they knew the Text inside and out. They may not have been great at living the commands, but they certainly could recite them!

Their intimate knowledge of the Word allowed them to speak to each other and quote it to each other in a kind of Biblical short-hand. Only referencing a part of a verse would be all that was needed for the Jew you were conversing with to know what you were saying.

Combining verses into one statement was also common, as the original versions of Scripture weren't handily divided into chapters and verses the way they are in our Bibles today. And even though Leviticus and Deuteronomy were certainly distinct works, the fact that they were both written by Moses and were both part of the Torah meant parts of one book were often quoted alongside other parts of another book.

WHAT NEXT?

If you weren't aware of that, however, and if you weren't familiar with the Old Testament text, you might read the Lawyer's answer here and think there was some verse in the Old Testament that contained everything he said. There isn't: It's two verses mashed together because the lawyer wasn't just quoting verses in a vacuum; he was interpreting multiple statements by the inspired Moses to answer the question Jesus posed him.

The lawyer was, in other words, using the whole counsel of God to shape His understanding. That's the way we're supposed to read the Bible. To that end, Bible students today should try to get away from seeing the Bible as a series of fortune cookie sayings, handily broken into 31,000 consumable portions (verses).

The Bible is sixty-six books, yes, but it is also one unified Text, with various divisions and sections that need to be appreciated in order to properly understand it.

Have you ever said, or have you ever heard someone say "I can't understand the Bible. It's too big. It's too complicated. I wouldn't even know where to start." First of all statements like that are very common and there's no shame in admitting it.

There have been many times I have read a text from my Bible and thought: "I have no idea what I just read." What I often ended up doing was reading it again, and again, sometimes going back to the original language, or looking at different translations of words, all in an effort to figure out what was being said in that challenging verse. Even then, I sometimes can't always grasp the reason or the meaning behind it. It happens.

The worst thing you can do is just throw your hands in the air and say: "well, I guess it can't be done...I can't figure it out." If that was truly the case, then it's not you that failed but the God who wrote it! If God wrote a Book that you can't understand, but your salvation is dependent on your understanding it, then God's got a problem. But I don't believe that's the case. I don't believe the Bible can't be understood. I think it can be, but sometimes we need a little push. We need to be steered in the right direction.

I think the biggest obstacle people have in understanding their Bibles is not in terms of reading and comprehending, but in terms of understanding the way the Bible is laid out. The Bible is not Harry Potter, where you have to start with book one, read it from beginning to end, then move on to book two, read it from beginning to end, and so on till you're done.

Sure, no one's stopping you from opening up to page one, Genesis 1:1, and reading all the

WHAT NEXT?

way until page whatever, Revelation 22:21, cover to cover, beginning to end. You're free to do that, but you're not going to understand God's Word that way. It's not a book like that.

In fact, if we're going to be really technical about it, the Bible is not even "just sixty-six books." The Bible actually contains books within books. There are thirty-nine books within the volume of the Old Testament, and another twenty-seven books within the volume of the New Testament. The Bible contains books within books within the Book, and those books aren't all one kind of book...

Some of them are history books.
Some of them are writings of prophesy.
Some of them are works of poetry.
Some are letters written to individuals.
Some are letters written to entire nations.

In all, there are sixty-six books written across different eras, by different people, in different languages, to different audiences, for different purposes. There is a unifying force at work (the hand of God), but when you zoom into it, sometimes it can be hard to see how and why the different books all fit together.

It can be a daunting undertaking to sit down with the Bible in front of you and say to yourself "I'm going to figure this thing out." Where do you even begin? In my opinion, you should begin by understanding the way the Bible is arranged. Starting there will help you know what to focus on as you read and study it in detail.

To that end, I have a handy chart I like to use as a simple introduction to the Bible. This breaks the Text into five components, showing the student how there are FIVE divisions of the Old Testament, FOUR divisions of the New Testament, THREE dispensations of time, TWO defined eras of history, and ONE dominant message that unites it all.

Understanding these five things will not explain everything there is to know about the Bible (you'll be spending the rest of your life trying to know everything there is to know, and you'll never discover it all), but it will help set you on the path for how to study and understand the Bible that God gave you.

Here's the chart...

WHAT NEXT?

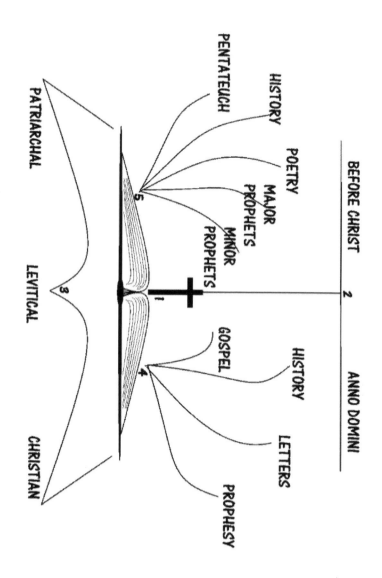

MATTHEW L. MARTIN

FIVE DIVISIONS
OF THE OLD TESTAMENT

The Old Testament is broken into a handful of genres. There are books of Law, History, Poetry, and Prophesy. Yes, those are only four categories, not five, but we'll get there.

To start with, there are the books of law. These are the first five books of the Bible, written by Moses, and are otherwise known as the Pentateuch. From Genesis through Deuteronomy, they inform the reader of God's creation and the first steps in His plan that would end with the cross of Christ and the salvation of humanity.

Genesis starts with the beginning of creation and ends with the focus being put on one nation—Israel—that had settled in Egypt. Exodus informs us of the captivity of Israel and their deliverance by God out of Pharoah's hand. Leviticus details the particular aspects of the Law God gave to the nation. Numbers lets us follow the people as they wandered in the wilderness. Deuteronomy gives us Moses' final speeches to the people before his death.

These five books follow one consistent narrative, but they're not history books like Joshua, or Samuel, because the scope is too large and broad to be classified in that way. Instead, these books are epics, telling the overall history

WHAT NEXT?

of the beginning of all things, and the choosing of Israel to be God's vessel to bring about the Savior of humanity.

After the Pentateuch are the history books. Joshua-Esther give us insight into the lives of this nation that is at the center of the Old Testament. That said, as you read these books, you'll soon notice that the narrative hops around quite a bit.

You start out following Joshua and the first settlers of the land of Israel, then you jump ahead to the time of the Judges, before jumping over to an entirely different land to study Ruth. After that, you go back to follow the lives of Saul, David, and Solomon, the first Kings of Israel, before all the rest of the Kings have their history chronicled in the remaining books of this section. The final books discuss the fall of the Kingdom into the hands of the Babylonian Empire, a deed done by God as punishment for their continued rebellion. That leads to the books of Ezra, Nehemiah, and Esther, who write about the people being in Babylon and Persia.

While the Pentateuch is big in scope, the history books are smaller in scale. Still, these books are important because key characters and events are mentioned here that are important to understand when you get to the New Testament.

After the history books are the poetry books, stretching from Job to Song of Solomon. Even though Job lived sometime in the period of Genesis (probably around chapter 12), his book is placed where it is because the style of its writing fits better with the other books of poetry.

The same is true of Psalms, Proverbs, Ecclesiastes, and Song of Solomon: We have those books, and they are valuable to us, either because they give us important information (the psalms are littered with prophesy of the Christ to come), or because we can use them to better understand something. My reading a love letter Solomon wrote doesn't do much for me, but applications can be made, and that **does** help.

After the poetry books are the prophetic books, which are, themselves, split into two sub-genres: Major Prophets and Minor Prophets. The former include the books of Isaiah-Daniel. The latter include the books of Hosea-Malachi. The difference in these two chunks of books are in the way they are presented: The major prophets are four-course meals; the minor prophets are finger foods. The two groups of books serve different purposes; one is big picture, one is small picture.

There are your five divisions of the Old Testament., and each one is very different in style, scope, and purpose. You can't just read

WHAT NEXT?

them straight through, cover to cover, and expect to understand it all. If you do, you're going to be all kinds of lost when you finish Esther and you wonder who this Job guy is. These books aren't meant to be **read** like a novel; they're resources meant to be **studied**.

FOUR DIVISIONS
OF THE NEW TESTAMENT

Like the Old Testament, the New Testament is broken into a handful of genres. There are books of Gospel, History, Letters, and Prophesy.

To begin with, there are the books of the Gospel, Matthew-John. These are not four Gospel books. There are not four Gospels. There is one Gospel. There is one message of Good News concerning Jesus' life, death, and life again. That one Gospel is told from four different perspectives, and to four different audiences.

Matthew wrote to Jews about the savior of the Jews. Mark wrote to Gentiles about the savior of the Gentiles. Luke wrote to an individual about the humanity of Christ. John wrote so that the reader could believe the deity of Christ. The four of them accomplish their own purpose, but they also complement each other in magnifying the greatness and the mission of the God|Man.

MATTHEW L. MARTIN

Unlike the Old Testament, the New Testament has only one history book, Acts. But where the Old Testament history books focused on the physical nation of Israel, Acts tells us the history of the spiritual nation of Christ's church.

An understanding of Old Testament history gives us perspective to help us understand New Testament history (when we read it, we see how God protected and punished the Old Testament nation as needed). By studying Old Testament history, we come to understand God's mindset to protect and punish, which carries over to His relationship with His New Testament nation, the church of Jesus Christ.

The bulk of the New Testament is comprised of letters, from Romans-Jude. Sadly, despite these books being the bread and butter of the New Testament, these are the parts that are so often overlooked in sermons across the country. These are the writings given to us to govern how we are to live and worship and be faithful to Christ.

When people say "I don't need to know what Paul said or what Peter thinks, just tell me what Jesus said..." they miss the boat entirely. Jesus left those Apostles in charge, and empowered them with inspiration to write these letters, first so that the early Christians could

WHAT NEXT?

know what God's truth was and how to follow it, and later for Christians who came after—us—to know and follow the same truth.

We **need** these books, and we need to study them as they are written. These are resource books, guides for us to relate to and make application from, so that we never have to wonder what is and isn't acceptable Christian behavior.

After the letters, there is one final book. It is a work of prophesy called "the revelation." The theme of the book is our victory in Jesus. Rightly is it the last book of the New Testament, as it was the last book written and because its message is so final and so conclusive, there's nothing else to add.

Don't worry what Satan may do to you; if you have Christ you have victory. You have that victory now and for all eternity. That's the message of Revelation, and it's a wonderful end to the inspired record.

There are five divisions of the Old Testament and four divisions of the New, each has its own purpose and focus, but they both come together to give us God's complete written instruction for man. It's up to us to rightly divide it (2 Timothy 2:15).

We do that, by understanding the next part of the chart...

MATTHEW L. MARTIN

THREE DISPENSATIONS OF TIME

In all of history, God has communicated His will to humanity, but He has expressed that will through different means. First, there was a patriarchal age, in which God spoke to each family on a case-by-case basis, as needed. Laws and commandments were given to each head of the house, the patriarch. For example, He told Noah to build a boat, but he didn't tell **everyone** that. He told Abraham to leave his country and start walking to Canaan, but He didn't tell everyone that. This was God's method of communicating with man as recorded throughout the book of Genesis.

But then, in Exodus, the focus moved away from a single person to an entire nation of the world. God became the God of the nation of Israel, a people whose purpose was to provide an environment from which the Messiah would one day come. All nations need laws to govern them, so God gave them a law at Mt. Sinai. The first ten of those commandments we're all familiar with, but a lot more commandments followed. And since this was a nation whose chief decision-maker wasn't a president or even a King, but was God Himself, the focus of the nation wasn't on a congress but on a priesthood. That's why this period of time is called the Levitical age.

WHAT NEXT?

The days of the Levites were replaced by the Christian age, in which Jesus rules over His spiritual nation, and gives us the law to follow today (His **new** covenant and testament). This is the age in which we live today, and when we study our Bibles we do so with the understanding that the authority for what we do and don't do comes from Christ, not from the Law of Moses or from the heads of our households.

It's important to understand these three distinct dispensations are found in the Bible. When a Christian says, "I can't do that; it's a sin," there will likely be someone ready to argue by saying "Well in Genesis they did it" or "in 2 Kings they did it!"

Those days are done. Those dispensations are passed. We are under Christian law now; that's what governs us. When you understand that, it makes reading and understanding the Bible a lot easier.

TWO DEFINED ERAS OF HISTORY

There was a time before Christ and there are the days **of** Christ. That's it. Those are the two ways to view history. Everything before Christ was leading up to the pivotal moment of Christ's arrival. It is **the** line of demarcation, not just in the Bible but in all of human history.

Everything that came before Christ immediately was looked at differently once Christ came to this world. For that reason, we must read those "B.C." books differently from the rest, because they served a different purpose from the books written in the age of Christ.

Those B.C. books were written simply to educate us, to prepare the world for the life God wants us to live in Christ. The rest of the Bible are the "A.D." books. A.D. is short for Anno Domini. It is **not**, as some mistakenly claim, short for "AFTER DEATH." The words come from the Latin, and mean "in the year of the Lord."

In those days, calendars were kept in line with whoever was the king of that land. A traveler could go to one nation and be told it was "the year 2" because it was the second year of their monarch's reign. You might journey two kingdoms over, however, and they would call it the year 29. There was no big-picture calendar like we have. Our calendar basically came about in the late 1500s, and it marks its beginning point with the birth of Christ (or at least tries to).

As of this writing, it is the year AD2022, also known as "the year of our Lord, 2022," or "the 2022nd year of His reign," since a King's reign was marked as beginning with His birth.

Just as everything in the B.C. era was building to a climactic point, everything in the

WHAT NEXT?

A.D. era is looking back on that same climactic point, the time when Jesus came into our lives, born into this world, to die for our sins.

Which takes us to the final piece of the Bible Study pie. There are five divisions of the Old Testament, four divisions of the New Testament, three dispensations of time, two divisions of history, and...

ONE DOMINANT MESSAGE
AT THE CENTER OF IT ALL

What is the one message of the Bible? What is the one thing God wants us to learn from a study of His word? It is that salvation has been brought down.

Listen to Paul...

> *This is a faithful saying, and worthy of all acceptation, that Christ Jesus came into the world to save sinners; of whom I am chief (1 Timothy 1:15).*

The one message of the Bible is this: We can have salvation through Christ. You may not understand every detail about the Bible. There may be parts that frustratingly elude you. There may be things you will **never** understand. Okay.

MATTHEW L. MARTIN

That's fine. You can still look at the big picture, and you can see how from Genesis to the end, your salvation was on God's mind.

That being said, it's important that you don't **stop** with just the basic understanding of God's desire to save you. You need to continue studying and learning God's will for you, but if you start with that fundamental truth, you will build your Bible study on the right foundation, and you will find it much easier to open the pages of the New Testament and begin a life as a "student" of God's Word.

And speaking of...

WHAT NEXT?

Chapter Eleven

HOW DO I STUDY
THE NEW TESTAMENT?

Despite the fact that the Bible is completed, with no more books being added and no more inspired words being penned—going back two-thousand years—it remains a work of "revelation" in more ways than one.

The Bible reveals the will of God, not only to the first-time reader, seeking to know the history of who we are, where we came from, where we're going, etc, but also it reveals the will of God to the fifty-year student of the Texts. The man who

WHAT NEXT?

has read the Bible, cover to cover, three hundred times, is just as likely to discover something he'd never considered before, as the man who first breaks the plastic wrap on a brand new Bible and opens it to read for the very first time.

The brilliance of written inspiration, as opposed to orally-transmitted information, is that it allows the would-be learner to pace himself, pouring over the words, absorbing them and meditating on them over the course of years, as opposed to the span of a conversation. God inspired many prophets to deliver orations of inspiration over the course of thousands of years, but all that remains of their Divine words are what was recorded with ink and pen.

People who read and re-read the Lord of the Rings over and over don't come away with a deeper understanding of self or of things greater than self. People who can quote Shakespeare as fluently as they can recall their home address don't feel such a connection to the words that knowing them sparks personal growth or enlightenment. They read and quote those things purely for social fun or academic flexing. On the other hand, the Bible continues to enlighten and those who have read it fifty times will argue that each time they've read it, a new discovery in one section brings deeper understanding in another.

MATTHEW L. MARTIN

This is remarkable, especially considering the fact that the Bible is not—unlike Lord of the Rings or Shakespeare's works—the work of one author, written within a single lifetime. As discussed in the previous chapter, the Bible contains sixty-six works, penned by some forty different writers, spread across fifty generations. Being able to identify a theme spread across that many books, written across that great a distance of time and space, is something that can only be done with the Bible.

As for the twenty-seven books that comprise the Bible's "New Testament," it offers the same opportunities for enlightenment, only compressed into a smaller package. The New Testament, while being in many ways the "second half" of the Bible, would be better viewed as a stand-alone product. That's not to discard the Old Testament or deny its (many) thematic and overt connections to the New Testament, nor is it to discount the fact that the New Testament is a collection of individual writings.

Instead, we should think of the New Testament as a series of books with an intended purpose as laid out by God. The Old Testament books have their own purpose, and the whole Bible likewise has a purpose, but strictly speaking of the New Testament, one does not need to read it fifty times to come away thinking "there is a

WHAT NEXT?

big picture here that God is trying to get me to see." Such a fact seems obvious after just the first read-through of the twenty-seven books.

That being said, some scholars might dispute that idea or argue that the New Testament has no central, unified theme. And yet, even those who would argue such must also concede that there is at least a dominant message that is pervasive through the twenty-seven books. That being said, if you are vague enough, you can find a "message" in any work, fictional or otherwise, even if one is explicitly not intended by the author.

Does the New Testament have a clear, precise theme that can be followed from Matthew through Revelation, or is it—as some critics allege—just a collection of books merely united around a vague theme like "salvation" or—the one right answer in every children's Bible class—"Jesus"? I have an answer, but so do many other writers...

DOES THE NEW TESTAMENT HAVE A UNIFIED THEME?

The scholar E.M. Stevens thought so. He said that the revelation of the New Testament was given so that man could know God's "plan of foreordination" and "the reality of man's redemption from Adam's sin through Jesus' reconciliation." The scholar Garland Elkins argued that the New Testament was inspired by God in order "to prove that the Lord loved, and that He died to prove His love." Both men promoted a unifying theme to the New Testament.

The scholar Alexander Campbell argued that the New Testament was a thematic work from the mind of a God who put themes and patterns into everything. He said that the New Testament's theme "speaks of man as he was, and also as he will hereafter be." He went on to say the New Testament "dwells on man as he is, and as he ought to be, as its peculiar and appropriate theme."

The scholar Thomas Warren argued that the theme of the New Testament is "to make Christians only...and the only Christians." The scholar Goebel Music wrote a whole book built around this idea, and even though his focus wasn't specifically on a "theme" to the New Testament, he still indirectly affirms his convictions for there being one. He argues that the New Testament was written to reveal "the promise of the church to be built by Christ, including its coming into existence." He wrote that the New Testament reveals "the unshakable kingdom which has now been, for ages, received, preached, and taught as

WHAT NEXT?

the body of Christ and as the way—and only way—wherein man could be saved."

I'm no scholar, but for my part, I think there's a theme to be found in the New Testament. I would argue the theme should be summarized in terms of God's relationship with man or, more precisely, how God reconciles that relationship. How does God reconcile the fact that He is utterly holy and we—due to our disobedience—have become utterly sinful? The answer: He reconciles it through the person of Jesus Christ, the God|Man.

Through Jesus Christ, we have redemption and justification. The New Testament is the collection of inspired writings meant to introduce us to Jesus, instruct us by Jesus (and His proxies), and motivate us to remain faithful for Jesus. The New Testament, as far as I am concerned, has as its theme: "All things related to our faith in, repentance to, confession of, baptism into, understanding from, and victory with Jesus Christ."

In other words, the New Testament was conceived in the mind of God to be the complete and ultimate (meaning "final") authority on the subject of our relationship with Jesus. Anyone, therefore, who offers something less than what the New Testament provides on that subject can be rejected immediately as offering less than the total amount available. Anyone offering more than what the New Testament provides on the subject can be rejected as offering material that goes beyond the "final" word on the subject. Anyone offering the same amount of material can be rejected too, since the sum-total that needs to be known has already been provided by God.

You can find something related to the aforementioned topics in every book of the New Testament, but you can also find some books which, either directly or indirectly, make those topics a priority and focus...

MATTHEW AND MARK PRIORITIZE BELIEVING IN JESUS

Certainly, the writer John makes it clear that his book is written so that we might believe that Jesus is the Son of God, but Matthew and Mark approach that idea from a different perspective. While John focuses on the Divine nature of Jesus as the Son of God, Matthew and Mark emphasize Jesus from the vantage point of the audiences they are addressing in their respective works.

Matthew writes for his Jewish readers to believe in Jesus as the Jewish Savior. Everything he writes is geared toward that end, and the specific moments in Jesus' life and ministry that he

WHAT NEXT?

includes in his work (by inspiration) are designed primarily to steer the Jewish reader into believing in Jesus as the long-awaited Messiah. This is why there are so many Old Testament references and allusions in Matthew's work, as opposed to the mere handful that the other three Gospel writers provide; Matthew is building a legal case for Jesus to be seen and believed as the Christ.

When Jesus came to the borders of Caesarea-Philippi (Matthew 16:13-17), He asked His disciples whom the general public believed Him to be. They answered that some thought He was a resurrected prophet (Elijah, Jeremiah, John the baptizer). Peter, however, knew better: He stated with conviction that Jesus was the "Christ" (meaning "anointed one" or "messiah").

Matthew places that moment almost exactly halfway through his writing and uses the first half to build up to that declaration, offering an inspired record on the miracles performed, the sermons taught, and the Old Testament prophesies fulfilled to make Peter's claim not so much a wishful-statement from a bought-in disciple, but a verifiable conclusion drawn from obvious facts. The second half of the book that follows Peter's declaration shows Jesus moving downhill toward the Jews' capital city, where their hatred and vengeance would culminate in the death of their Messiah, only for Him to be resurrected with a new purpose: To rule as King over a new Kingdom, one for Jews and Gentiles.

Mark's book is written to those very Gentiles. Though it's still a biography of the Jewish man, who lived among Jewish men, and whose illustrations and sermons were often Judeo-centric, the angle of the Roman writer is to show Jesus as a Savior for non-Jews to believe in too. Just before He ascended into Heaven, to rule as King, the Lord committed His disciples to the task of spreading the news about His death, burial, and resurrection. In that commission, He ordered the Gospel to be spread to "every creature" (Mark 16:16).

Within the greater theme of the whole New Testament, Matthew and Mark offer books to impress upon their reader the global invitation of God: The whole world can be saved by Jesus, the whole world needs to know about Jesus, and the whole world has the right to believe in Jesus. The first two books of the New Testament make the distribution of those facts their principal aim.

LUKE PRIORITIZES
REPENTING TO JESUS

Of course, Luke's writing is concerned with many spiritual topics beyond repentance, but it's worth noting that this particular subject

WHAT NEXT?

is peppered throughout the writing, to a degree not found in Matthew, Mark, or John's Gospel Accounts. In Matthew, you can find eleven instances of the word in varying forms. In Mark, the word is found four times. In John it's absent entirely. Luke, however, uses the word thirteen times.

Notably, Luke uses the word in describing the overall Ministry of Jesus, saying He preached the baptism of repentance for the remission of sins (Luke 3:3). The Lord Himself describes His ministry as one that calls sinners, not self-righteous ones, to repentance (Luke 5:32). Luke is the only writer to record Jesus' famous declaration that one sin is not lesser or worse than another because all must repent or perish (Luke 13:1-5).

Luke is also the only writer to include the three powerful "parables of the lost and found." At the end of the first two, Jesus reflects on the joy found amongst God and His angels when one sinner repents (Luke 15:7, 10), and then devotes the third to the whole concept of repenting and being forgiven, despite not ever using the word to describe the "prodigal son" (Luke 15:11-32).

The discussion of the Rich Man and Lazarus is recorded only in Luke's account, and it ends with Abraham's reminder that a sinner who didn't want to obey the Word of God would not repent, even if confronted by someone who rose from the dead (Luke 16:30-31). Just one chapter later, Jesus challenges us to be a forgiving people, saying that if our brother sins against us even seven times in a day, but repents seven times as well, we should extend mercy to him every time, just as God the Father would do to us when we repent (Luke 17:3-4).

Finally, at the end of Jesus Christ's time on earth, as the Lord prepared to ascend into Heaven, Luke's writing comes full circle. He began with Jesus "preaching the baptism of repentance for the remission of sins," and he ends with Jesus committing His disciples to the same great charge, preaching "repentance and remission of sins" in His name, beginning at Jerusalem (Luke 24:47).

If there's ever a text that highlights Luke's emphasis on repentance more than Matthew and Mark, it is that Great Commission account. All three of the synoptic writers include the moment when Jesus gives His final command to the Apostles, but while Matthew and Mark's accounts are extremely similar (Matthew 28:18-20, Mark 16:15-16), Luke's is notably different. He doesn't say a variation of "go into all the world and preach the Gospel" but instead has Jesus telling them to preach "repentance and remission." That's what he was concerned about in his book.

WHAT NEXT?

That's the aspect of Jesus' Ministry that he put under the spotlight.

Within the greater theme of the whole New Testament, Luke offers a book meant to impress upon the reader the desire of God to be reunited with His people: Sin separates us from God, and while it is Jesus who personally reconciles us back to Him, Luke reminds us of the personal responsibility all people have in sinning. We chose to abandon God and, thus, we must choose to return. Repentance is that choice, and Luke's book emphasizes that fact.

JOHN PRIORITIZES
CONFESSING THE DEITY OF JESUS

To be clear, the Apostle John expressly states the purpose behind writing his book: "These (miracles of Jesus) are written that you might believe that Jesus is the Christ, the Son of God, and that (by) believing, you might have life in His name" (John 20:31). And yet, what does God want me to do with the belief I have in Jesus? What does anyone do with the convictions they have? They proclaim them!

In fact, there's almost a sub-theme that runs throughout the New Testament, when you focus solely on John's four contributions to Holy Writ. All of his texts feature the deity of Jesus—

His Godhood nature—being explored either in great or small detail. His first epistle and this Gospel account in particular seem to have been written to combat the Gnostic heresy that, among other things, reduced Jesus either to a mere mortal man or some quasi-"lesser god."

While Matthew, Mark, and Luke took great pains to illustrate the humanity of Jesus, with mentions of His hunger, temptations, disappointment, and so forth, showing Him to be a true "son of Man," John wants His readers to see Jesus as more than a Man: He is "God in the flesh" (John 1:14).

It's not enough to confess your belief that Jesus lived, because everyone who has ever been has lived. It's not enough to confess your belief that Jesus died, nor even that He rose from the dead. After all, the Bible has numerous references to people being resurrected after death; those risen people aren't Messiahs to be worshipped. The Divine Nature of the Man Jesus needed to be directly argued.

When Peter made the great confession (Matthew 16:18), Matthew put the emphasis on the Christ-hood of Jesus. Most who recite the verse leave off what came next: Jesus told Peter that his confession was made because of the Divine work Peter had been witness to, as opposed to any physical/flesh-and-blood proof

WHAT NEXT?

(Matthew 16:19). And even though there are many miracles recorded in Matthew's Gospel (and in Mark and Luke's accounts, too)—with any of the three books having more miracles recorded than John's Gospel—those supernatural moments are not the focus of the writing.

In John's Gospel, at least in the first half, the miracles take center stage. John's book can be split into two equal parts. In the first half, John singles out seven miracles Jesus performed, highlighting the Lord's compassion, His authority over nature, and His power over death. By the time you read the seventh miracle (the raising of Lazarus from the dead), there can be no denying the Divinity of Jesus. In fact, John helps the reader along to that conclusion, showing how—following Lazarus' resurrection—even the Religious Leaders plotting against Him could not deny His power (John 11:47).

In the second half, John slows down the pace and focuses exclusively on the Lord's final hours. As a matter of fact, over three-quarters of John's final chapters (thirteen through nineteen) examine only a single twenty-four-hour period (the arrest, trial, and execution of Jesus). There is so much more to the life of Jesus that John chooses not to explore; that information can be studied in the books written by Matthew, Mark, and Luke, which succeed in presenting Jesus as a

MATTHEW L. MARTIN

Savior for both Jew and Gentile to believe in and repent to. John's aim with his writing is different than those three: His focus is on showing that Jesus is the Son of God: sent from Heaven, confirmed by miracles, killed for our sins, and risen to reign as our King.

In John's final chapters, he describes the final days of Jesus' ministry and how everything that happened to Him was done according to God's plan, to achieve the salvation of our souls. His miracles are seen in the first half; His Deity is confirmed as a result. All that's left for Jesus to do is die for us and rise for us, doing for us what no mere mortal could: Redeeming us.

At the conclusion of John's book, the writer tells us that the testimony recorded therein is true (John 21:24). He should know since he was an eyewitness to it (1 John 1:1). He also says that there was much more that Jesus did which he did not record, since it would take more books than the world could contain to write them all (John 21:25). And yet what is written was written for a specific purpose, and that purpose is more than just for our personal, introspective belief.

Within the greater theme of the whole New Testament, John offers a book meant to impress upon the reader the Deity of Jesus and the unique nature He held as the God|Man. The

WHAT NEXT?

text seeks to instill in its readers a testimony of Truth in their hearts; a testimony which cannot remain internal, but which must be confessed before men.

ACTS PRIORITIZES
BEING ADDED TO THE KINGDOM OF JESUS

Throughout the book of Acts the reader follows various preachers on various evangelistic campaigns. Peter and John labor in Jerusalem, preaching to Jews. Philip takes the Gospel to Samaria, preaching to half-Jews. He also, by the counsel of God, seeks out an Ethiopian proselyte. Paul travels all over the world, from Jerusalem to Rome and back again, declaring the Death, Burial, and Resurrection of Jesus.

Despite the great variety of preachers to be studied in the book, as well as the vast discrepancy of audiences who hear the message, there are two constants that do not change throughout the book: First, the Gospel is the Gospel, and though the approach might change from sermon to sermon, the core message of the Gospel does not, no matter the audience. Second, those who obey the Gospel do so by being baptized into Christ.

In the beginning, Peter's sermon convicts his Jewish audience of the murder of the Messiah.

MATTHEW L. MARTIN

In his conclusion the Apostle tells them to repent of their horrible sins and be baptized for forgiveness (Acts 2:38). Later, Peter would take the Gospel to the Gentile Cornelius, and preach a much different sermon in tone and content. Despite that, when it came to the end, the conclusion and call to action was the same: Peter commanded them to be baptized (Acts 10:47-48).

In Samaria, the evangelist Philip delivered his message to an audience with far less blood on its hands than what Peter's Jerusalem audience had. Philip tells his listeners about the kingdom of Jesus, open to all men, and convicts them into belief. The sermons of Peter (on Pentecost) and Philip were no doubt similar but different in the emphasis. Nevertheless, in the end the result is the same: The Samaritans were baptized into Christ (Acts 8:12).

Paul's sermons largely eschewed talk of Jesus' Messianic nature, due to the predominant Gentile crowds he addressed. Nevertheless, after preaching on the miracles of Jesus, and declaring the Lord's resurrection and coming judgment, Paul's sermons contained a call for the believer to be baptized. That includes Paul himself; when he made his way, blindly, into Damascus, he was commanded of Ananias to begin anew by being baptized (Acts 22:16).

WHAT NEXT?

When Lydia heard the message of Paul, she responded with baptism (Acts 16:13-15). When the Philippian Jailor sought salvation, Paul pointed him to belief in Jesus and then to the baptistery (Acts 16:30-33). When Crispus of the synagogue believed Paul's teaching, he responded to it by being baptized (Acts 18:8). When the mistaught disciples of Ephesus learned the Truth from Paul, they—despite having already been baptized (improperly)—obeyed rightly by being baptized under Jesus' authority.

Over and over in Acts, the Bible reader can see the Message of Jesus being delivered to racially and ethnically diverse audiences. The angles and emphases in the various sermons change depending on the crowds, but the end result is the same: Those who believe Jesus as preached to them, those who repent to Jesus, and those who are convicted by the Divinity of Jesus, are baptized into Jesus to be saved by Jesus.

Acts works as more than just the second half of Luke's Gospel account; it's the book that puts all three Gospel texts into action. Throughout Matthew, Mark, Luke, and John, we read about Jesus' Ministry from the point of view of Jesus Himself. Only occasionally do we leave His point of view and only then to glean from the mindset of His enemies. In Acts, all that Jesus did and taught is delivered to audiences who did not know Jesus, did not spend years loving Jesus, and did not witness the resurrection of Jesus.

Within the greater theme of the whole New Testament, Acts offers a book meant to show us the power of the Gospel Message and its ability to convict and convert someone who has never met Jesus of Nazareth. How does such a person come to Christ? How are they permitted to enter into Christ's holy Kingdom? They are told of Jesus' Gospel, and they obey it in baptism. That's the formula. We know it is because Acts lays it out, clearly, for us to see.

THE EPISTLES PRIORITIZE
THE FAITHFULLY-FOLLOWED DOCTRINE
WE RECEIVED FROM JESUS

It seems almost inappropriate to try and fit twenty-one books—over three-quarters of the New Testament—into one thematic box. Of course, if the whole New Testament can be thematically summarized, why not part of it? The Gospel accounts serve to instill in the readers a belief in Jesus, a desire to repent, and an understanding of His Deity. Acts shows what the proper response to that belief and repentance should be, namely baptism into the kingdom of Jesus.

What then? After going through the first five books of the New Testament, the reader

WHAT NEXT?

should hopefully be a member of the New Testament church, but what does that entail? What are the expectations for those members? What are the rules and regulations? What are the practical bits of wisdom that new members need to learn from older ones? In other words, how are we supposed to live faithfully in Jesus? What do we need to do, and how are we supposed to be, in order to be faithful till death?

Romans provides a scholarly emphasis on the mechanics of justification. How did the holy God maintain His holiness while offering a salvation agreement to unholy man? You can argue that Romans is maybe too deep and heady for a novice Bible student, especially as the first epistle in the New Testament, but the text works in its placement by providing a doctrinal foundation for the relationship between God and man.

The next eight books are much more practical in their approach, offering the reader a steady stream of scenarios and solutions over a spacious spectrum of spiritual subjects. Everything from church discipline, to eschatology, to charitable giving, to the doctrine of Christian joy is discussed. Paul argues for salvation by grace through faith on one hand in Ephesians, and vehemently against proto-Gnosticism in Colossians on the other hand. He gives history lessons in 1 Corinthians, and impassioned defenses of both himself and the whole Apostolic group in 2 Corinthians.

Things get personal in the letters to Timothy and Titus, but the content is no less inspired or critical to the Bible student than the others epistles. Brethren seeking to know what kind of men are to shepherd them spiritually can find in these books the inspired qualifications for bishops. Brethren seeking to know what kind of preaching to look for (and avoid) can find in these books the inspired criteria for godly evangelism.

Hebrews works as a companion to Romans, not in content so much as in form and presentation. Like Romans, Hebrews is a meticulous, focused, doctrine-heavy book. If Romans is an inspired thesis on justification, Hebrews is one on how Christianity is the fulfillment of all the promises and plans given throughout the Old Testament. It's a critical book for Christians to understand in order to recognize their place in the eternal scheme of God.

The last of the epistles offer both general wisdom to specific audiences and specific wisdom to general audiences. James writes generally, about a host of practical subjects, to brethren specifically under persecution. John writes

WHAT NEXT?

specifically about Christianity in contrast to the Gnostic viewpoint to a general audience of believers. Peter's two letters, as well as Jude's, are general in both subject matter and intended audience. All seven of those letters contain important information for Christians concerning how to live, how to endure, how to serve, and how to love as the Master once did.

All of the epistles were written in the latter half of the first century, some coming as late as the 90s A.D. Their audiences were Gentiles who converted to Christianity thanks to the missionary efforts of Paul, or Jews who became disciples of Jesus through the teaching of Peter and John, etc. They were not the men who walked and talked with Jesus; they came later, almost all of whom never laid eyes on the Man they call Messiah. They didn't hear His sermon on the mount. They didn't see his raising of Lazarus. They didn't sit at His feet while He expounded parables. They didn't watch Him endure hatred and mockery with meekness and mercy.

Nevertheless, through the Gospel accounts, those readers were shown the way of Jesus. Through Acts, those readers were shown the pattern of obedience. Through the epistles, those readers were shown the expectations of holy living. They didn't have to be eye-witnesses to know how to live soberly and righteously in their present world; they had the inspired epistles to guide them.

Christians today, two-thousand years later, have the same luxury. Like those first New Testament readers, we didn't walk in the shadow of Jesus, and unlike those early brethren, we didn't even have the privilege of sitting at the feet of the Apostles. Despite that, the infallible Word guides us, and what instructed brethren then still instructs us now.

Within the greater theme of the whole New Testament, the epistles provide Divine instruction for how to live faithfully in Jesus Christ. Though diverse in topic, audience, scope, and authorship, the twenty-one letters in the middle of the New Testament offer all the doctrinal instruction we need to live and serve as our Father in Heaven intends.

REVELATION PRIORITIZES
THE HEAVENLY VICTORY
WE HAVE WITH JESUS

Scholars, commentators, Bible students aged and new all love to debate the minutiae of Revelation. Everyone loves to get into the weeds and debate the details or focus on the trees to the ignoring of the forest. While it is good to dig

WHAT NEXT?

deep and learn as much as can be about any subject—particularly a Biblical one—it's also important not to forget the overall message in each book of the Bible. Especially when it comes to a book like Revelation, it is paramount that the overall message not be forgotten. A book with so much coded messaging and illustrative imagery needs first to be grasped at the "big picture" stage before a study of the particulars can be addressed.

What is the big picture message of Revelation? The answer to that is also the answer to why it's the perfect book to close out the New Testament. Revelation is not the "end" of inspired canon simply because it was last written. In fact, there's no definitive proof it was the last-written book (any of John's three epistles might've been penned later). No, Revelation closes the Word of God because the men who compiled and collected the sixty-six volumes of the Bible recognized its overall theme was appropriate as the last thing you would read before finishing God's Message.

What is the theme of Revelation? It is this: If we have Jesus we have victory. What better way to end a Book whose single message is the life, death, and life-again of Jesus! He attained His victory early in the New Testament when He rose from the grave. Where is our victory? It is in that

MATTHEW L. MARTIN

same empty tomb. It is in the promise of resurrection and life-unending. Armed with that assurance, the disciple of Jesus can face any obstacle. He can stare death in the face and sing his way to the chopping block. Revelation gives him that confidence. Revelation assures him of his victory.

Within the greater theme of the whole New Testament, the book of Revelation is not about Nero or Domitian. It's not about Dragons in the sky or what the meaning of the "sea" is. The theme of Revelation is victory, and when viewed in context with the rest of the New Testament, that theme is understood as the final victory we achieve after a life of faithful living in Jesus.

It is important when studying the New Testament to appreciate the fact that you're reading twenty-seven unique books, all united by the Holy Spirit's inspiration, and all working together to serve a single unifying theme. What is that one message of the New Testament? It is the answer to the question: How can I, a sinner of earth, have a spiritual relationship with the sinless God of Heaven?

That question is answered in Matthew and Mark, who introduce me to Jesus, in whom I believe. It is answered in Luke, who teaches me about repentance and the need to turn away

WHAT NEXT?

from self and turn to Christ for forgiveness. It is answered in John, who reveals the Divine nature of Jesus, which I confess to the world.

It is answered in Acts, which provides the template for my obedience. It is answered in the books from Romans through Jude, which counsel and instruct me on how to live in this new, spiritual life I now enjoy. And it is answered in Revelation, which promises undeserved victory in exchange for humble service and faithful living.

The New Testament is God's plan for my salvation in Jesus. That is its theme: Bridging the gap between the holy hand of God and the sinful hand of man through the death, burial, resurrection, and promised second-coming of Jesus Christ.

With the basics of the New Testament established, now comes the tricky part...

Chapter Twelve

HOW DO I INTERPRET THE NEW TESTAMENT?

Unfortunately, whenever I read a passage of Scripture that I don't quite understand, I don't have the luxury of calling the Apostle Luke and asking him what he meant when he wrote *this* verse, etc. I am left with a book, the authors of which are long dead, that I must study and understand in order to have eternal life.

Fortunately, the God who gave me that book also gave me a brain, common sense, and an ability to grow and learn and make sense of complex things. To that end, while it can sometimes be daunting to stare at the giant book in front of you, keep in mind that God inspired it

WHAT NEXT?

to be written in such a way that anyone can understand what they need to know to be saved and to get out of this sinful world for good.

A critic of the Bible might try to say that the mind of God is so vast and so unknowable that it is arrogant even to think that we could understand His Bible. Nonsense, I say: Is God smart or isn't He? Am I to believe that God isn't smart enough to write something that I can understand? Are we really going to say that God gave us a Book, knowing we couldn't understand it, and commanded us to study it anyway? Is He just toying with us?

No. God's mind **is** vast, but it is, in fact, so vast, He is able to take the unknowable things of His mind and make them knowable to us through His inspired writers. In fact, Paul specifically says as much (1 Corinthians 2:7-13).

And yet, we still have to put in the work. We still have to study. We still have to use our brains and our common sense intellect to grasp the things contained in the Bible.

There are commands to be found in the Bible, commands which we are expected to obey. Those commands are sometimes plainly and directly stated. Sometimes they are seen by authoritative example, and sometimes they are implied. However they are presented, they are inspired and expected to be obeyed.

MATTHEW L. MARTIN

First of all, the things spoken by the Apostles are the commandments of the Lord. That's what Paul says (1 Corinthians 14:37). We can't "just read the red letters of Jesus" and be okay. Jesus gave the Apostles the authority to lead His church. Biblical authority is necessary for a religious act to be acceptable, and that authority can be found, sometimes, via direct statements in Scripture.

DIRECT COMMANDS

What is a "direct statement" of Scripture? For one, it's not just a commandment. For example, Mark 16:16 does not contain an imperative command, but it is a declarative, and from it we can discern that we need to be baptized. Matthew 7:21 isn't a command either, but it contains expectations of things to be done (doing the will of the Father); that's imperative-esque. 1 John 1:7 tells us that we must walk in the light to have fellowship & forgiveness, despite the fact that it never actually tells us **to** walk in the light. We have brains and the ability to apply reading comprehension, however; we know what John meant.

Are there plainly stated commands in the New Testament? Certainly: Acts 2:38 contains one given by Peter ("repent and be baptized").

WHAT NEXT?

Acts 22:16 does as well, given by Ananias ("arise and be baptized"). 1 Corinthians 11:24 has one, given by the Lord via the Apostle ("Do this in remembrance"). Paul plainly says "lie not" in Colossians 3:9. Peter plainly says "desire the word" in 1 Peter 2:2. The point is, those aren't the only ways the New Testament writers give us commands.

There are also interrogative commands in Scripture that inform us with rhetorical questions, such as Romans 6:1, which asks the question "shall we continue in sin that grace may abound?" The question implies the answer (no we shall not). Paul actually writes it out in the next phrase, but he didn't need to; it was understood just from the way he phrased the question.

Paul also asked the question: "Don't you know that sinners won't inherit the Kingdom of Heaven" (1 Corinthians 6:9-10). The phrasing implies the answer; no, sinners won't inherit the Kingdom.

There are also so-called hortatory ("let us") commands that imply an action must be done. Let us press on toward spiritual maturity (Hebrews 6:1). Let us motivate each other to do good works (Hebrews 10:22-25). Let us walk honestly (Romans 13:13). There are many of these in the New Testament, and none of them are

MATTHEW L. MARTIN

intended to be optional suggestions. These are commandments without a plainly stated "thou shalt" or "thou shalt not" attached to them.

CULTURAL COMMANDS

Sometimes the New Testament contains a command that must be done, but the "way" in which it is done is left up to the person or culture to define. For example, Paul commands us to greet one another sincerely, not hypocritically. How one greets another changes over time and across cultures. In the time and place of Paul, a kiss on the cheek was a common form of greeting, thus Paul commanded the brethren to greet one another with a "holy" kiss, as opposed to an unholy one (an insincere or unloving greeting). We cannot command a kiss-greeting, but we are commanded to greet as Christians should, with sincerity and love.

The New Testament speaks frequently about modesty: That's a command (be modest). In the first century of eastern Europe, modesty meant women not having braided hair. It meant wearing veils over their faces. That's cultural. The command to be modest, however, in whatever form that takes, is universal.

To prove that, consider how in one text Paul says being modest means having braided hair (1 Timothy 2:9) and, in another text to a different audience, commands women to be veiled (1 Corinthians 11:5). Here's the thing: A "veil" in that culture was more akin to a burka; it covered the entire head, meaning there would be no way to see the woman's hair. In other words, in cultures where a woman had to wear a veil to be modest, it was irrelevant whether or not her hair was braided. In other cultures, it mattered. There is a universal command (be modest), and it is applied culturally.

GENERIC COMMANDS

Our Master commands Disciples to go into all the world and make more Disciples (Matthew 28:19). How did the early Disciples do that? They walked and occasionally rode horses or mules. Do we have to do that? No, because the command "go" is generic. How it is carried out is left to the discretion of the one obeying.

Paul commands us to do good to all men (Galatians 6:10). How do we do good? That's up to us. So long as it is good, the command is obeyed.

EXAMPLES

We interpret the New Testament by understanding the commands it gives us, not only when those commands are stated, but also when they are provided by example. In other words, just by observing how brethren lived, we can follow their template and live as they lived, being faithful as they were faithful.

Christ expected people to follow the teachings of the inspired Apostles (Matthew 16:19, John 15:26-27), and the Apostles taught not only with word but also with deed. They told and they showed. They commanded and they left examples for us to follow. The Apostolic example was intended to be followed (2 Thessalonians 3:6).

In fact, the best verse to summarize this point shows Paul plainly saying we must follow his example...

> *Brethren, be followers together of me, and mark them which walk so as ye have us for an ensample (Philippians 3:17).*

The Apostles were Jesus' inspired, authoritative ambassadors on earth. Their entire mission was to lead the church in its early days, guiding the brethren (present and future) about what they could and could not do. They did this not only with stated commands, but also by showing as opposed to telling.

When we read, for example, about Peter being rebuked for showing Jewish favoritism over

WHAT NEXT?

Gentiles, we learn by example that such actions are wrong (Galatians 2:12). When we read about the Corinthians being shamed for not withdrawing their fellowship from an unrepentant brother, we learn by example the when and why to withdraw our fellowship from erring brethren (1 Corinthians 5:1).

When we read that the Disciples came together on the first day of the week to worship, we learn by example that we too must meet on the first day of the week (Acts 20:7). That being said, when we read that they met in an upper room, that part is optional. Why? Because brethren didn't always meet in an upper room, but they did always meet.

Because of the role the Apostles played in establishing patterns for brethren to follow, the first Christians did not play fast and loose with the Apostolic pattern. They recognized there were not just direct commands, but also examples to emulate. When we study the New Testament, we have to follow that same mindset, looking not only for the commands that are stated, but the ones that are shown, as well.

IMPLICATION / INFERENCE

Does God hold man responsible for what He implies in the Scriptures? Yes. While there are people today who try to argue otherwise, the fact is the Bible implies things to be done and things to be abstained, and God expects us to use the brains He gave us to understand those various implications.

It's very convenient for a false teacher to argue that if the Scriptures do not specifically forbid something then it's okay to do it, when that very liberal approach to command-keeping is not applied anywhere else in life.

If your mother tells you to play in the backyard and later finds you in the front yard, will you be punished for disobeying? Yes. What if you try to say "well you didn't say **not** to go to the front yard"? What happens then?

You'll be punished again for being sassy.

We use implication in our command-giving all the time. It's a basic function of language, and since God uses language to communicate with us (especially the written language of the Bible), it is not only understandable but expected that He would use implication in His command-giving.

The fact is, however, directly stated commands are easily understood. Examples, once you figure out how to spot them, are easily understood, as well. Inferring commands from

WHAT NEXT?

implication takes a bit more elbow work from the Bible student, which is probably why the whole concept is so frequently attacked.

Consider some common examples of implied commands: First, God told Noah to build the ark with gopher wood and to build according to specific measurements (Genesis 6). Those commands imply no other type of wood or measurement was acceptable. Noah, therefore, inferred that he should only use gopher wood and that he should design the craft to meet the exact specs provided by Jehovah.

The priests Nadab and Abihu were killed by God for offering strange fire on the altar (Leviticus 10). In fact, the writer specifically says they offered fire God did not command them to use (Leviticus 10:1). Did God specifically tell them **not** to use that fire? No. He merely said where the fire was supposed to come from, thus implying that all others were forbidden. The priests were supposed to infer the command. They did not. They died as a result.

Uzzah reached out and touched the Ark of the Covenant, to prevent it from falling off the cart that was carrying it. Upon touching it, he was struck dead for handling a holy thing without permission (1 Chronicles 13:9-10). The only instruction regarding touching the Ark comes from Numbers 4:15, which offers no direct commands or prohibitions. All we're told is that Aaron covered the Ark a certain way so as not to touch it. All we have is a simple, matter-of-fact statement, but it implies that the Ark was not to be touched. Uzzah was supposed to infer from the implication that he would be punished for touching the ark. He did not. He died.

The case of Uzzah is especially noteworthy because, unlike Nadab and Abihu, Uzzah's heart was in the right place. He meant well, yet because he did the wrong thing, he was punished. Lesson learned: God cares about you doing things the right way, **and** He cares when you do the wrong thing, too, regardless of your motive.

A law does not have to detail everything it **doesn't** allow. To go back to the illustration of a mother and child: If your mother sends you to the store with some money and a command: "go to the store for milk," and you come home with milk and candy, you will be punished. What's the crime? Stealing. You took her money and bought something she did not command you to buy, and the only reason you are guilty of stealing is because that command was implied.

If you order "pepperoni pizza" and the delivery person brings you a pizza with pepperoni and pineapple, you will be angry. Think about this: There is a false teacher out

WHAT NEXT?

there named Rubel Shelly, who says that we don't have to look for implied commands in the Bible. But I will bet you a nickel that Rubel Shelly would complain if his pepperoni pizza had pineapple on it. In other words, Rubel Shelly has more respect for a pizza than he does the Bible.

God expects you to **study** to learn what is a command, example, implied doctrine, or just a random factoid that has no bearing on your life. God's Truth requires research. You can't be lazy and unconcerned about the Bible and expect to follow it correctly. That kind of attitude is why some people follow the preacher and not the Bible, and are led right off the edge into error.

Does God not intend for us to understand his sometimes-challenging Book? If we're not meant to understand it then why write it? If we are meant to understand it, then we must study to learn it. Why did God even give us revelation the way He did? Maybe it's because He wants to separate the true seekers from the lazy.

God absolutely holds people accountable for not learning. Jesus commanded the people to "go and learn..." (Matthew 9:13). Paul wrote that he expected us to understand the will of the Lord (Ephesians 5:17). It isn't always easy, but it can be done.

MATTHEW L. MARTIN

Sinners continue to make up their own ways to interpret God's Word. In fact, it all started with the Devil doing just that: "You will **not** die" he lied (Genesis 3:4). What God wants us to do is defend His revelation for what it is, and not tolerate the manipulation of His word.

God wrote the Book. He provided within it commands, examples, and implications. By studying and interpreting the Bible in the way it was written, we not only learn what is expected of us, but also what rewards are waiting for us on the other side of life.

WHAT NEXT?

Chapter Thirteen

WHAT IS MY "THEOLOGY"

Especially for those living in the so-called "Bible Belt of America," there are church buildings full of believers found everywhere you look. Granted, you don't have to limit your search only to the southern USA; the New England area is replete with beautiful, centuries-old church buildings and cathedrals, many of which are well-attended, especially around religious holidays.

There's a bit more zeal to be found in the South, however. Here, while you can find so-called "mega churches" with tens of thousands of members, most of the time what you see in town after town are small church buildings, with

WHAT NEXT?

enough seating to hold a hundred people, occupied by close to a hundred people week in and week out.

Believers are everywhere. It reminds me of what Paul said when he visited Athens, and observed that the people are notably religious and very devoted to their gods (Acts 17:2). You cannot walk down a main street in a typical Southern town without finding at least two handfuls of church buildings, and of those church buildings, you will be hard-pressed to find any two that share the same doctrine.

Are there commonalities? Sure. They will all profess Christ is the King. They will all speak, in one way or another, of the evils of sin. They will express hope of life beyond this one. Yet, when you get to the details, the differences begin to show themselves.

As a result of so much religious division, there's a question that is commonly asked, one we've talked about already in this book: "What kind of Christian are you?" It's not a question that would ever have been asked in the days of Peter, Paul, or John, because their era of Christianity was not so divided. Paul was not a particular kind of Christian; Paul was just a Christian, and those whom he taught and baptized were "just Christians," too.

MATTHEW L. MARTIN

What the person today means when they ask that is: "What do you believe?" They want to know the way in which you understand the Bible. They want to know whether you agree or disagree with one particular hot-button issue or another. What they're asking you, even if they don't use the word, is "what is your theology?"

They're not asking in **whom** do you believe, because your answer is Jesus, the same as theirs. Nevertheless, despite that commonality, the one asking the question understands there are fundamental differences between you. That difference is in "theology."

To that end, your theology must be the New Testament. Others will point to the revered writings of scholars like Calvin, Luther, Thomas Aquinas, Smith, or Wesley. They will hold up the teachings of well-studied men who examined the New Testament and wrote essays on how best to interpret it.

Do you see the flaw there? You were not baptized into the name of Calvin, however. You were not taught the Gospel of Wesley. Thomas Aquinas did not die on the cross for you. Studying the writings of smart people is rarely a bad thing. Relying on them as the basis for one's faith **is**.

What is your theology? Are you a Wesleyan Christian or are you a New Testament

WHAT NEXT?

Christian? The former is a diluted brand of Christianity, one that has been run through the filter of a man merely commenting on the inspired writings of Jesus' Apostles. The latter is someone who submits only to the words of inspiration, and uses the teachings of men merely as a help to better understand the Text of God.

There's a big difference between reading the words of men to better understand a verse of Scripture, and taking those words of men as the basis for an entire religious sect. What did you study to obey the Gospel? The New Testament. Thus, what is your theology? Your answer better be the same: The New Testament.

The heart of your Christian theology is understanding how Jesus is revealed by God to the world through the inspired writings of the New Testament. In that case, if that is your theology, then you ought to be studying it. You ought to know the New Testament as much as a citizen of a country ought to know the laws of the land where they live. When you do, you'll not only be able to explain to someone what you believe and why, you'll also be prepared to answer them when they challenge you on their theology of men vs. your unfiltered theology of the New Testament.

Consider this chapter a summary of the New Testament, to help new Christians get their feet wet in understanding the wider world of Bible study they will be diving into for the rest of their natural lives. There are twenty-seven books in the New Testament, and though each of them are unique, they are all inspired by the same Holy Spirit, and thus all fit together to form a unified narrative and theme.

Though the books may have different authors, audiences, reasons for writing, and other societal circumstances happening around them, reading and studying only one offers but a fragment of the knowledge that the Bible student is supposed to have.

That being said, there are disadvantages to thinking of Matthew as "chapter one of the New Testament" or Revelation as "chapter twenty-seven." That sort of mentality leads us to look for connections that the original authors perhaps didn't intend.

What did the inspired Paul mean when he rejoiced over "salvation through faith without works" (Ephesians 2:8-9)? It's different from what the inspired writer James meant when he condemned "salvation through faith without works" (James 2:24). When we treat the New Testament as a kind of stew, with twenty-seven ingredients all intended to be blended together, we do a disservice to ourselves as Bible students

WHAT NEXT?

and to the Holy Spirit who inspired twenty-seven separate but equal works of Divine insight.

Within each book of the New Testament exists a self-contained thesis, explored by that inspired writer, drawing from that writer's personal insights, educational background, cultural standing, etc, all to service the greater purpose of making the one studying the Word complete and completely furnished to do every good work (2 Timothy 3:16-17).

If "theology" is about understanding God, and "New Testament Theology" about understanding how God's Son is revealed in the New Testament, then each book of the New Testament ought to offer separate but equal contributions to our greater understanding of God (and, particularly, God in Christ Jesus).

Indeed they do...

MATTHEW

Matthew was a Jew, whose audience was primarily Jewish, who wrote a very Judeo-centric book, about the Jewish Messiah. Thus, Matthew reveals in his book the God of Abraham, Isaac, and Jacob, whose Messiah has come to save Israel in the personage of Jesus. The book is laid out perfectly, with opening chapters that establish the Divinity and authority of Jesus, middle

MATTHEW L. MARTIN

chapters that present the sermons and miracles of Jesus, and closing chapters that highlight the death, burial, and resurrection of Jesus.

The text begins with a genealogical record connecting Jesus to Abraham. Why not start with Adam, as Luke does? Beginning with Abraham puts the focus on Jesus' fulfillment of God's promise to the Patriarch that through his seed would all families be blessed (Genesis 12:1-3). After that, the birth of Jesus is shown from the perspective of Joseph (the Messiah's surrogate father), as told by the angel of God, before the threat of Herod against him is described in language highly evocative of Moses' Exodus account. The timeframe jumps ahead to the Lord's baptism and subsequent temptation, before Matthew devotes three chapters to the Lord's Sermon on a Mount, a didactic discourse tour de force on His Kingdom and her citizens.

With the opening completed, Matthew has established where Jesus came from and what Jesus came for; the middle of the book verifies those claims with various miracles described, parables taught, and rebukes against religious leaders handed out. By the time the reader arrives at the final third, he has come to know and believe the Messianic nature of Jesus. All that's left is to present a vivid account of His unjust arrest, unfair trial, unconscionable torture, and unparalleled death, burial, and resurrection.

Matthew's book reveals to a Jewish audience how the Jewish Jesus fulfills the prophesies of their Jewish history, to be the Jewish Messiah they long-awaited. Can the book be appreciated by Gentiles? Naturally it can, but theologically and contextually, it's a Judeo-centric work.

MARK

Unlike the Jewish Matthew, Mark was a (half) Roman, and his writing accommodates the Roman preference for shorter, snappier stories. Mark's Gospel account is the briefest of the four, streamlining many of the synoptic events and offering almost nothing in his biography that can't also be found in the other three (two miracles are recorded here that aren't found elsewhere). Likewise does Mark abstain almost entirely from quoting Old Testament texts, doing so only once at the beginning of his writing (Mark 1:2-3).

Also unlike Matthew, Mark's book lacks a strong and obvious outline. He omits the birth narrative and nearly all of the Lord's sermons, opting to focus on big moments in the ministry of Jesus. He highlights miracles and prophesies without any discernable pattern for most of the text, before spending the final few chapters on the Lord's death, burial and resurrection.

Nevertheless, Mark's account is critical when viewed in the context of the writing. Assuming that the text was written in the mid-60s (and that is the common belief), the church of Christ would have been in the midst of a period of tremendous persecution under Emperor Nero. A book biographing Jesus as the Jewish Messiah is good and all, but something snappier, quicker to the point, and focused on the big points of import to Roman Christians (Jesus' holy anointing, miraculous power, salvation-promise, and glorious resurrection) would be vital to those suffering brethren. Mark's book reveals those big points and offers hope to the church in Rome and beyond.

LUKE

Being the longest of the four Gospel accounts, Luke takes his time walking the reader through the ministry of Jesus. He has more sermons than Matthew, more parables than Mark, and more miracles than John. If you take away the Old Testament references that populate the book of Matthew, Luke's account has the most original material of the three "synoptic" accounts. Its length is not a detriment, nor is its placement as the third of the three synoptic biographies. You might think, after reading Matthew and Mark, that you've read all about Jesus that needs to be said, but then you move on to Luke and find something new on almost every page.

With Matthew and Mark, the Bible student must read between the lines to understand what the book's primary intention is. Luke, on the other hand, states his intentions at the outset of his writing. His purpose was to record the history of Jesus' ministry as revealed to him by eyewitnesses, and to present those facts in order, compiled together into one package. His text was addressed to the Greek Theophilus who, being a Gentile, likely would have been unfamiliar with Matthew's text. Furthermore, being a Greek, he likely would have had less interest in the many Old Testament annotations than a Jewish reader might.

Luke, therefore, wrote the Gospel for a Gentile audience, revealing the person of Jesus as the savior of humanity, irrespective of culture, language, ethnicity, or history. In that respect, it's fitting that Luke would spend more time than the others on the humanity of Jesus. He devotes extra time to the Lord's earthly birth (even tracing his genealogical lineage back to the first man), offers the only inspired account of his adolescent days, highlights the prayers, moments of grief, and words of rebuke more than the others too. Jesus is the Jewish Messiah; that much is established by Matthew. He is the one executed by Romans but glorified by God; that's Mark's message. He is also the Man acquainted with grief, full of compassion, preaching repentance, and committed to seeking and saving the lost; that's Luke's depiction of the Christ.

JOHN

John stands apart from the other Gospel writers. Not only is this book different because it came about much later, when most in the Christian world would have had access to the writings of Matthew, Mark, and Luke, but also because the purpose for the writing is the most singularly focused of the four.

John's purpose in writing was not to retread the well-covered ground of the synoptic accounts, but instead to supplement those writings with new information and descriptions of acts performed by Jesus. Indeed, roughly three-fourths of John's book is unique to it. Whereas Matthew, Mark, and Luke often overlapped and presented similar accounts in their writings (such as Jesus calming the Galilee storm), John not only

WHAT NEXT?

provides new information, he leaves out much of the old.

To that end, it is interesting to note what John does not include in his writing, which Matthew, Mark, and Luke offer. There is nothing in this writing about Jesus' birth or early life. There is no genealogical record provided. Nothing is written at all to describe Jesus before His baptism, at which point His ministry began. There is no mention of Jesus' temptation after His baptism nor of the transfiguration of Jesus on the mountaintop (an event the author was present for, according to Matthew). There is little mention of scribes or publicans; nothing is said of the Sermon on the Mount. There are no parables to be found.

Instead, this writing contains tremendous new information. The purpose of the book is not to lay out a step-by-step recitation of Jesus' life, or even of His three-year ministry, but instead to highlight the proof that Jesus was the Son of God. Whereas Matthew, Mark, and Luke wrote "proactive" Gospels, with the impetus on them to explain Jesus, in their own styles, to their own audiences, John wrote a "reactive" Gospel, in order to remind the Christian world that Jesus was not just a Man but was God in the flesh. That was a doctrine and a Truth that had come under attack by Gnostics in the late-first century, making it a timely and important focus on the part of the writer.

Thus, the book focuses on seven specific miracles: turning water into wine (chapter two), healing the nobleman's son (chapter four), healing the lame man at Bethesda (chapter five), feeding five thousand (chapter six), walking on water (chapter six), healing the blind man (chapter nine) and raising Lazarus (chapter eleven). Three miracles show His power over nature (turning water into wine, feeding five thousand, and walking on water). Three miracles show His compassion (healing the nobleman's son, the lame man, and the blind man). One miracle shows His power over death (when He raised up Lazarus).

Each of those seven miracles, and later the arrest, trial, execution, and resurrection of the Lord—all of which are contained in this letter—constitute only about twenty days in the life of Jesus. A whole third of the book (chapters thirteen through nineteen) examines only a single twenty-four-hour period. This book must be studied, not as a biography, but as a sermon; the purpose of which, unequivocally, is to show that Jesus is the Son of God. That literary purpose, by the way, is specifically stated by the inspired author (John 20:30-31).

WHAT NEXT?

All books of the New Testament are critical, and no study of "New Testament Theology" can be complete without a study of all twenty-seven volumes, but if there was one book that might stand out as a "pocket New Testament" that succinctly summarized what Christ and Christianity are all about, it would be John's magnificent text.

ACTS

Acts serves as a direct sequel to Luke, following up the former writing in a way like no other book in the New Testament. Paul's letters to Corinth and the preacher Timothy both had second installments, as did Peter's letter; John wrote two additional letters after his first epistle, but none had such a feel of "part two" as this one. As Luke's Gospel account ends, Jesus is ascended into Heaven and the disciples return to Jerusalem to await the power He will send from Heaven. Acts begins almost with a "previously on..." before diving into a history of the establishment and early days of the Kingdom of Jesus.

In that respect, Acts serves as a bridge between the Gospel accounts that open the New Testament and the many epistles that will follow. The opening chapters lay out the details of when

MATTHEW L. MARTIN

and how Jesus' many Kingdom-prophesies and promises came to pass. They take a movement that, to that point, had been centered around a single Man, whose Disciples were largely unknown, and expands it from Jerusalem, to Judea, to Samaria, and finally to the greater Gentile world.

In Acts, we follow the ministry of Peter and, later, Paul, as well as read about many of the conversions that became the foundations for the epistles that are later sent. If "New Testament Theology" is the study of God and how He interacts with man, then Acts is a tremendously important book to study from a theological perspective, as it takes all of the doctrines, principles, and lessons we learn, not only from Jesus' earthly Ministry, but also from the Apostles' letters that followed, and shows us how ordinary people put them into practice.

It's one thing to read about Jesus telling us to rejoice and be glad when persecuted (Matthew 5:12) or to read Peter write the same message (1 Peter 1:7), but it affects us in a different, more powerful way, to read Peter actually being persecuted and rejoicing as His Master taught him (Acts 5:41). That's the power of the book of Acts, and that's why it's such a critical book in a study of New Testament Theology.

WHAT NEXT?

ROMANS

The book of Romans is arguably the seminal work of Holy Writ. The subject matter from its inspired author, the Apostle Paul, is one of justification and reconciliation to God through the blood of Christ. The theme of the book answers a question asked by Job thousands of years earlier: "How shall a man be just before God?" (Job 9:2).

Paul rigidly outlines the text, breaking the letter into three distinct parts. Chapters one through eight discuss the origins of justification (and, in fact, those chapters can be divided themselves into two groups: [1] What justification is not, and [2] What justification is). Chapters nine through eleven discuss the globalization of justification. Chapters twelve through sixteen discuss the application of justification. The first eight chapters are doctrinal, the next three are conversational, and the final five are practical.

This epistle is not a personal letter; it is a treatise: It is an essay on the subject of justification. It is not a love letter from one to another; it is a work of scholarship, from the most scholarly and intellectual man ever to pen an inspired book. In it, Paul argues that salvation is the same for both the Jew and the Gentile, that both are equally guilty of sin and worthy of death, and that to both is extended the mercy of God. Jews in those days believed they were saved because they were Jews. In this letter, Paul explains why that is not the case, and that salvation actually comes by way of Christ's undeserved justification.

No scholarly study of New Testament Theology can be complete without a detailed look at the book of Romans, as it is the most scholarly and meticulously-argued book of the whole New Testament, if not the whole Bible itself.

1 CORINTHIANS

If it's doctrine you want, the first Corinthian epistle has it in spades. Without question, the brethren at Corinth faced a myriad of problems. In fact, one could argue that if a person needed a pattern for a congregation that wrestled with every breed of doctrinal squabble, the church at Corinth is your template. In Paul's first of these two inspired letters, he writes and addresses the problems this congregation faced.

As you read through them, you will notice that many of them are challenges brethren of the twenty-first-century struggle with. Some of them are specific to the time period, certainly, but even then the roots of the problems are sins that are

WHAT NEXT?

commonplace today (selfishness, division, a lack of love, etc).

A common misconception exists concerning the first-century church: There are those that look at the Lord's body in the first century and say the church then, despite the persecution, had it easier than brethren have it today. After all, they say, the church then had the Apostles to take care of all the little problems that existed. Nonsense: Today, like in the first century, there exist congregations struggling with doctrinal problems.

Though we don't have Apostles in the flesh to correct our mistakes, we do have the Apostles' doctrine to help us be faithful to God. In light of that, a doctrine-heavy book like this is indispensable, not only for learning but for an understanding of New Testament Theology, since it's through obedience and faithfulness that we have a relationship with God in Christ.

2 CORINTHIANS

The cause for this second inspired letter to Corinth, which is said by the Apostle to have been written about a year after the previous letter (2 Corinthians 8:10), is hinted at in the tenth chapter: Paul talks about the false teachers (Judaizers) who had infiltrated the congregation there. The Bible student will recall that in First Corinthians, Paul indicated a desire to visit Corinth as soon as possible. Instead, he was delayed (and delayed). As a result of his delaying, in his absence, Paul's enemies spread lies and slanderous things about him. They called him weak and cowardly; they called him a liar and someone inferior to the other Apostles. As a result, Paul is forced, not only to defend himself, but also the church at large and the Christ who appointed him an Apostle over it.

When studying the second letter, especially immediately after a study of the first, it's important to remember that this is a different letter, not a "second half." Though the author and its original audience are the same, the content and the reason for its writing are totally different. As such, the feel of the letter is different from the one that preceded it. The first epistle was very organized, with Paul breaking down a series of problems and offering spiritual solutions, one after the other.

The second letter feels, at times, more like a personal letter than a doctrinal one. Nevertheless, there is plenty of doctrine to discuss, despite the letter's structure being less intellectual and more personal. A study of it, therefore, is highly beneficial to the Bible student seeking to learn, not only pure doctrine, but also

WHAT NEXT?

New Testament Theology, examining the personal hurt that false doctrine can have on God's teachers, and on God Himself.

GALATIANS

Based on Paul's arguments, it is clear that the challenge facing the Galatian brethren was the need to remain loyal to Christ and His Law and not be carried away by false teachers. These false teachers were arguing that the New Testament alone was insufficient; they were Jewish by nationality and had converted to Christ, yet refused to abandon many of the precepts of the Old Law of Moses. These "Judaizers" sought to bind Old Covenant commandments onto their Gentile brethren. Specifically, they argued that salvation for a Gentile was dependent on circumcision. Paul argues against this and shows what purpose the Old Law held, and how that purpose was fulfilled and finished with the giving of the New Law.

Paul argues that Gentile Christians are just as much the recipients of the Abrahamic blessing as were the Jews. Likewise, he illustrates the weakness of the Old Law with the allegory of Sara and Hagar. A reading of the text, therefore, indicates that the letter was intended to be received by a mixture of Jew and Gentile readers.

MATTHEW L. MARTIN

In the book's six chapters, Paul establishes the fact that salvation comes by faith in Christ (in conjunction to obedience to His Law) and not by the Law of Moses. To argue that fact, Paul (1) rebukes the Galatians for falling for the attacks against the Law of Christ, (2) defends the Law of Christ against those attacks, (3) shows how the Old Law was fulfilled in the New, (4) explains the need for the Law of Christ to those who are attacking it, and (5-6) makes application to the brethren from those arguments.

Like Romans, Galatians is a doctrine-heavy book. The purpose behind the writing is threefold: (1) Paul argues for the validity of his Apostleship against those who were seeking to discredit it. (2) He illustrates the all-sufficiency of the New Testament as the only presently-approved Law from God to man. (3) He exhorts the brethren to serve each other, while providing practical advice on a variety of topics. As he moves through each topic, the New Testament Theology of the writing shines forth as Paul defends the Doctrine of Christ as the only way to have a relationship with God.

EPHESIANS

Ephesians is best viewed as a companion to the epistle to the Colossians and a contrast

WHAT NEXT?

(though not contradictory) to the epistle to the Galatians. Whereas the Galatian letter emphasized the "Law" of Christ (in contrast to the Law of Moses), this letter focuses on the "body" of Christ, His church. The tone of the letter is also different from Galatians in that it is more general in topic, with little "hard doctrine" being debated. Instead, the Apostle focuses on the various blessings to be had within the body of Christ. To that end, the Apostle uses a phrase in this letter that is not found anywhere else in the New Testament: "heavenly places" (referring to the Throne of God, the dwelling place of God's blessings, and blessed people).

Nevertheless, though the tone of the letter is not as doctrinally-focused as some of the other letters by Paul, there can be found, throughout the six chapters, an outline to follow. The Apostle opens the letter with a discussion of the blessings found in the body of Christ (chapter 1). From there, he turns to the sense of family that belongs to the body of Christ (chapter 2). He then discusses salvation, which was once an Old Testament mystery, but is now fulfilled in the body of Christ (chapter 3).

A discussion of unity in the body of Christ drives the next portion of scripture (chapter 4), before the Apostle turns his attention to the kind of love that is housed within the body of Christ (chapter 5). The final portion of the letter is devoted to the need for brethren to stand up and defend the body of Christ from outside attacks (chapter 6). Because of the uplifting nature of the writing, in spite of the external circumstances of the author, there are few other texts which are as able to bring joy to the reader as this. Since theology is the study of God and His relationship to man, a book whose primary focus is on the blessings of that relationship is an important one to study, theologically.

PHILIPPIANS

Few books are so therapeutic as Paul's letter of comfort, contentment, and joy to the Philippians. Even the origins of the writer's relationship with the region provides a great lesson to learn: Before Paul and Silas' work, the missionary labor of God's people had never extended into Europe.

As Paul traveled on his second missionary journey, he sailed from Troas across the Aegean Sea to the European city of Neapolis (Acts 16). From there, he and Silas traveled ten miles North to the city of Philippi. Along the way, he converted a Gentile woman named Lydia and healed a woman possessed (Acts 16:14-16). The result of the latter work landed the Apostle in a

WHAT NEXT?

Philippian prison cell. Did such distress deter the Apostle and his companion? On the contrary, they began their imprisonment with some singing and ended with the conversion of the jailer (Acts 16:23-34)!

A decade later (around A.D. 62-63), a thriving congregation of the Lord's people was meeting regularly in Philippi. The Apostle Paul once again found himself behind bars and thus pens this letter. In it, he writes of the joy he finds in Jesus Christ, and encourages his brethren to have the same measure of joy. Without necessarily spelling that out, the Apostle—in writing about his present predicament without the slightest hint of frustration—explains how Christians are to live: Joyful children of God are a part of a church which is thankful (chapter one), sacrificial (chapter two), committed (chapter three) and virtuous (chapter four).

Likely, the Bible student can read the book of Philippians in about half an hour, but the lessons learned from it—as Paul expounds on the joyous life a child of God has and the privilege of God's people to suffer for the name of the King—will lift the spirits forever, and keep you coming back to it time and again, during both good days and bad.

MATTHEW L. MARTIN

COLOSSIANS

The circumstances behind the Colossian letter are important to know if one is to have a complete understanding of the epistle. Colossae had become a breeding ground for many false teachers and false doctrines. In fact, many of today's most prominent false religious doctrines (associated with Christianity) began in this city around the time of this letter's writing. Paul's purpose in writing was to encourage his brethren to stay loyal to inspired Truth as well as rebuke the error that was permeating from their city.

Unlike Philippians, the content of the book is inundated with doctrinal statements, explanations, and commands. Because of that, the tone of the letter is sharper than the Philippian letter, though not as harshly rebuking as his earlier Galatian epistle. There seemed to be two individual false teachings that had infiltrated the minds of brethren in the area. The first was the oft-debated Judaizing problem: Jewish Christians were binding circumcision on their Gentile brethren, and Paul writes to refute the need for a physical surgery to justify a redeemed soul.

The second doctrine was a kind of proto-Gnosticism. The many false teachings of Gnosticism are refuted here, decades before the movement fully formed. Among the false ideas

WHAT NEXT?

Paul combats is the teaching that flesh is evil and man is inherently bad. That untruth led them to conclude that God (Who is inherently good) must not have truly created man, and therefore He (being what they called the "Demi-God") used various others ("little gods," of which Jesus was but one) to create all things (Paul actually refutes this in Ephesians 1:23).

Likewise, in thinking all flesh is evil, they concluded that Jesus could not have come bodily and that He must only have been a projection, merely **appearing** to be flesh-and-blood. In addition, they taught that, because the body is evil and the soul is good, the two are so incompatible that a person can do whatever he wishes with his body (such as sin) and his soul not be jeopardized. That false teaching still exists today, though Paul sufficiently refutes it in this two-thousand-year-old letter!

Paul refutes each of these premises and more in the body of this letter. Along the way, he points out the all-sufficiency of Christ as head over His church. Each of the four chapters describes the Christ, with various descriptions given to Him as they relate to His church. He is depicted as Head of the church; He is shown to be the head of the new church, head of the risen church, and head of the faithful church. He is all we need and with Him only, every false doctrine falls by the wayside, withers, and dies. Just as Colossians effectively defeated false doctrines of Paul's day, the book is still effective in defeating modern false doctrines today, making a study of it paramount from a theological perspective.

1-2 THESSALONIANS

The writings of Paul's two letters to the Thessalonians are often overlooked when it comes to detailed, theological studies. There are a few very famous verses that receive a lot of attention, but the letters as a whole are typically passed over for meatier studies from larger New Testament books. This is a shame, because even though the two letters are brief, they offer tremendous knowledge to the reader.

Both books have an almost exclusive focus on one seminal event: The Second Coming of Jesus Christ. They take, however, different approaches in their discussion. The first letter is a very traditional Pauline epistle; the Apostle introduces himself to the reader and then spends a few chapters slowly building toward the primary aim of his writing.

With the first letter, it is not until chapter four (near the end of the text) that the writer digs deep into the subject matter, although the reader will spot hints and references to it in the

WHAT NEXT?

three preceding chapters. When it comes to 2 Thessalonians, the flow of the letter is the opposite of the first: Paul dives in on his subject almost immediately and uses the end of the letter to tie up loose ends.

The first epistle approaches the subject of the second coming primarily from the standpoint of the "resurrection." The brethren at Thessalonica apparently had a few misunderstandings about the event, and had come to believe that the second coming was a spectacle reserved only for those alive to witness it. Paul clears that up by explaining how the resurrection of the dead fits in with the return of the Lord.

In the second epistle, the subject is handled in a different way; that of "rest." The brethren were under attack from persecutions without and false teaching within. In order to provide comfort, Paul reminds his readers that the Second Coming of Jesus will be the day when all troubles will forever end. It will be the day when the saved will be at peace and the unrighteous enemies of God's people will be separated from them forever.

There are few Christian doctrines more fundamental than those related to the "final things." As such, there are few New Testament books more important to know inside and out than the Thessalonians epistles.

MATTHEW L. MARTIN

1-2 TIMOTHY & TITUS

Timothy and Titus were two of Paul's closest companions. Timothy was the young preacher mentioned frequently in the Book of Acts as a missionary alongside the Apostle, and Titus is mentioned in Paul's various congregational epistles as a fellow laborer with him. To them, Paul writes a total of three letters so full of doctrine and theology, they remain essential reading for all New Testament Christians.

The young preachers addressed in the texts received their letters from Paul soon after the Apostle was released from prison (and not long before he was re-arrested and eventually killed). Titus was left to help oversee the Lord's church on the island of Crete, and Timothy was to do likewise at Ephesus. The letter to Titus and the first letter to Timothy fit together nicely, having a similar style and function: They are written to give the recipients words of instruction and counsel and general encouragement. The second letter to Timothy, however, stands more on its own as a large portion of the text revolves around the imminent death of Paul.

What you don't find in these letters that you do find in other epistles from Paul are

WHAT NEXT?

rebukes and doctrinal discourses. These letters are different in form and function to the ones written to, say, Corinth or Galatia. These letters have doctrine, of course, but they are more personally stated than in any of Paul's other writings. The reason is obvious: He's not writing to a church; he's writing to friends.

Again, there is a lot of doctrine to be found here, but the way the material is presented is different from the way it is handled in other letters: Paul is not instructing a congregation on how to live; he's instructing a preacher on what to preach. Nevertheless, you don't need to be a preacher to appreciate the texts; you only need a desire to learn what kind of things a preacher should say; all Christians need to know that, which is why these books are critical to study in the field of New Testament Theology.

PHILEMON

When one abstractly examines the writings of Paul, it would be easy to overlook the letter to Philemon. It is tucked away, out of place between Titus and Hebrews, sharing little in common with either. It is Paul's shortest letter in the New Testament, but if we learn anything from a study of the Bible, it's that little is much when God is in it! Do not assume that a small letter is worth less consideration than a lengthier one.

Paul uses the fundamentals of Christianity itself to appeal to Philemon. The master of this run-away slave may be legally justified to exercise punishment on his subordinate, but Paul writes of the moral consequences of heartless, lawful punishment. They are no longer simply "master and servant;" they are now "brothers in Christ." As brothers, they are encouraged to reconcile spiritually, as that life is more important than the physical (1 Corinthians 6:7).

This letter is important. Though it is small in scope, private in prose, and largely devoid of doctrine, it is a must-study for all those seeking to find practical application for some of Christianity's most important concepts. How important is forgiveness? How important is repentance? How important is it for brethren to treat each other like family, despite sharing no earthly relation? These are the fundamentals that (in part) define Christianity, and they are at the core of this brief letter.

HEBREWS

The message of this book is of primary importance to the Christian. What good is the simple brilliance of James or the deep, engrossing

WHAT NEXT?

material in Romans if the Christian's own commitment to Christ is lost? What does it matter if 1 Corinthians is wall-to-wall doctrine—explaining and expounding a checklist of sins and their solutions—if the reader doesn't see his faith as worth maintaining in the first place?

Hebrews is a book written to Christians who have long heard the teaching of Christianity's fundamentals. The recipients of the letter knew the "ABCs" of their religion, but because of a lack of heart, they were being pulled away from their faith and were being tempted to leave Christ. They were being pressured to return to the seemingly easier life they had before they obeyed the Gospel.

The content of the letter leads to a conclusion that the audience was primarily Jewish-Christian. The thrust of the letter itself speaks to this end as the focus of the writing is on encouraging the reader to stay faithful (implying the recipients were brethren).

To make this point, the writer uses arguments from the Old Law to show the superiority of Christ's way over the Israelite faith. Thus it is reasonable to conclude that the readers were not simply familiar with the Hebrew faith but had a legitimate stake in its existence. Considering that the largest audience of Jewish-Christians maintained a residence in and around

Palestine, it is widely regarded that the readers were Jerusalem-dwelling Hebrews, previously Jewish by faith and now members of the kingdom of Christ.

The Christians to whom this book is written needed assurances that the Christian way is not only the better way but the only way available for them to have a right relationship with God. Thus the writer uses the Old Testament itself as the basis for his argument that Christianity is better. By showing that with each of the things the Jews hold up as worth preserving, God had in His plan a New Testament equivalent, one that is superior to the Old Testament version in every way.

Hebrews accomplishes the condensing of the some-4,000 year history of the Old Testament to show it all to be a prelude to the era of Christianity. Everything from the promise to Abraham, the brief appearance (and disappearance) of Melchizedek, the uber-specific rules and laws that comprised the Law of Moses and the entire creation and sustaining of the nation of Israel was designed to prepare the world for the Christian age.

If one was thinking of leaving the religion of Christianity for the religion of Judaism, here is a book that spells out in eight specific ways that Christ is—by God's design—better than the Law

WHAT NEXT?

and customs established in the Old Testament. It's a must-study for anyone seeking to grow their understanding of "NEW" Testament Theology.

JAMES, 1-2 PETER, 1-3 JOHN, JUDE

The inspired letters fitted between Hebrews and the book Revelation should be of great interest to all Bible students. The first comes from James, the content of which stands as a minor masterpiece. In this epistle, James warns of the dangers of—among other things—empty faith, the power of the words, and the presumption of Godless planning. His five-chapter book is so chock-full of wisdom and practical advice, it is rightly dubbed "the Proverbs of the New Testament."

In addition, there are two letters written by the Lord's most infamous disciple. Peter was the man who frequently blurted out whatever was on his mind, and as a result, he was commonly rebuked, yet he hardly wavered in his faith. The Apostle would himself grow and mature, eventually becoming a bishop in the Lord's kingdom. The older, wiser Peter, in his first epistle, writes about courage and hope in the face of persecution and adversity. His second letter focuses on the second coming of Christ and our need to remain faithful while mockers and scoffers reject the notion that Jesus will come again.

And then there are the three tiny epistles of John. They are often overlooked because the Gospel account and the Revelation letters penned by him are too often considered more worthy of study. But a mere reading of the letters provides a wealth of spiritual insight. John writes, among other things, to remind us that we can know our salvation is genuine.

Finally, there is Jude. He calls himself the brother of James, and thus it is reasonable to assume he is the half-brother of Jesus and brother to the author previously mentioned. His writing is interesting in that it came about as a result of some Divine intervention. He had intended to write about one subject, but the Spirit instructed him to instead write about something else. Thus Jude writes about the need for brethren to contend earnestly for the faith.

It is sad that so many of these writings (along with the other Bible books near the end of the New Testament) are frequently ignored by Bible Class teachers. In many assemblies, the books are overlooked, commonly skipped over on Sunday morning and Wednesday night classes, in favor of "another" study of the Gospel accounts.

WHAT NEXT?

While it is critical that we have a firm understanding of the life and ministry of Jesus, we must also be aware that such study is akin to a baby drinking milk. Milk-and-bottle feeding is vital for newborn babes, but it can't remain the diet of a Christian; more must be added. As Christians mature and grow in the faith, they must likewise graduate to eating strong meat, leaving the milk-and-bottle behind. A study of these "end of Bible" books, and the theological truths they teach, needs to be done more often if Christians are to grow into the kind of mature servants God would have us be.

REVELATION

Revelation can be understood. Common sense tells us that God would not go to the trouble of inspiring a text only to have its intended meaning forever remain a mystery. Is the writing in this book easily understood? No, to be blunt it is sometimes frustrating; the interpreter will often find himself certain that he has a phrase understood only to find his assumptions challenged (and sometimes obviously contradicted) by a phrase that appears later in the letter.

Revelation is not written like other books of the Bible. It is hard to understand at times

MATTHEW L. MARTIN

because that was the author's intention. Unlike the Gospel accounts, or Paul's letters to Corinth, or the general epistles of James or John, Revelation was written under circumstances where its content would have been screened by anti-Christian authorities. It was necessary, therefore, to tweak the material so that its intended audience could understand it while its unintended audience remained bewildered.

Even though the details of the book are harder to nail down, what is clear is the overall theme of the writing. No matter the date, it's clear God's people were in the midst of intense persecution. No matter your interpretation of this particular bit of imagery or that particular bit of metaphor, it's clear that John's message is "hang on, don't give up, because Christ has won the war. Hold on till the end and you'll be a victor with Him." Rome was breathing down the necks of God's people, but John was writing a secret word of encouragement, willing them over the finish line of faith.

With that in mind, we return to the original statement: Revelation can be understood. If it was written so that the Roman authorities would be confused and the Christian readers would be encouraged, that implies that John intended for his Christian readers to understand

223

WHAT NEXT?

his various metaphors and symbolic imagery in order to be encouraged.

Trying to understand the individual metaphors of the book is often like trying to put together a jigsaw puzzle without looking at the box. You can be told: "The puzzle is of an ocean with a green-sailed boat under a stormy sky." That's a general idea of what the picture is, but without being able to actually see the picture you're in the dark about the details: How big is the boat? Where is it in the picture? Is there lightning?

Without the picture, you're forced to lay down each piece, one at a time, trying them all until you find two that fit together, and sometimes pieces you thought fit together end up not, and you have to remove them and move them and try them somewhere else.

Revelation's big picture idea is "victory in Jesus." The fact that win and Satan loses is the message John is conveying here, and though Bible students might disagree on the particulars, we should all agree that the Bible ends its inspired record with a definitive assertion that those who serve on the side of Christ will be rewarded forever, and those who defy Him will suffer unendingly.

MATTHEW L. MARTIN

New students to the Bible might look at the twenty-seven books in front of them and feel like they're about to start a 1,000-piece jigsaw puzzle without the picture provided for them. The mistake comes in trying to study all twenty-seven books at once, or even all twenty-seven as though they were meant to be covered in turn, in order of printing. If you try to study the Bible that way, you'll be searching for its theological message with one hand behind your back.

The best way to eat an elephant is one bite at a time. Pick a book, read it and re-read it, learn its theme, and see how the author develops that theme throughout that one writing. Then do that again twenty-six more times. When you're done you'll feel like you've accomplished something...until you start over and learn things the second time you never considered in the first place. That's when you'll realize the Bible is a wondrous paradox: It's a book that was finished two-thousand-years-ago, yet keeps revealing new theological information to its readers and students every time they examine it.

WHAT NEXT?

Chapter Fourteen

WHAT IS CHRISTIANITY?

This will be the final "traditional" chapter of the book. The actual last chapter is a series of "lightning round" topics and thoughts to end with, but in terms of detailed discussions, this chapter is the end.

I can think of no better "last question," in that case, than the one that a new convert probably has never thought to ask, in so many words. Nevertheless, it's a question that needs to be answered and needs to be contemplated for the rest of our lives on earth.

What is Christianity? That's the question you have to ask yourself. Even though you can probably give a reasonably good answer right now without giving it much thought, it is good to pause and contemplate just how big a question this is, and how often the answer can help you as you live your life.

Whenever you're faced with troubling news, whenever you're confronted by a difficult temptation, whenever you're in the midst of a harrowing trial, whenever you need to repent of a terrible mistake, or whenever you need to tell someone else why they should take up the cross and follow Jesus just as you've done, the answer to this question—"What is Christianity?"—will be on your mind.

Any time you extend to a lost person the invitation of Jesus, you're essentially making a sales pitch. It may be the first of many, or it may be the one and only opportunity you'll ever have to talk to that person. Either way, when you tell someone about Jesus, you do so with the understanding that most people have a short attention span, and you will need to tell them something that is enticing and memorable enough to make them stop what they're doing and ask you to tell them more.

I say that to say this: Christianity itself is an invitation. The crux of the religion is to live a life that serves as an invitation for someone to leave what they know and become part of something new. In that case, it's our responsibility not just to bring the message of Jesus to people but to make that message enticing.

When we live hypocritical lives—saying one thing and doing another—we make Christianity a joke, and we make the invitation of Jesus a punchline. The things we say and do reflect the decision we made to put on Christ in baptism. The only way we are ever going to reach someone else with the same Gospel that reached us is if we live faithful to that Gospel and to the Christ who died to save us with it.

Think about it like this: If you could distill into one sentence what it is that makes Christ enticing, what would you say? In other words, if you only had one sentence to say, and one life showed everyone else that you truly lived by that one sentence, what would you say to entice someone to become a Christian like you? Here's what I would say:

To know Him is to love Him.

To me, that phrase is enticing. It's a little mysterious; it implies there's something about this Person that, if you experienced it, you'd be hooked: "If you knew this Person the way I do, you'd fall head over heels for Him, just as I have." That's the kind of comment that gets people

WHAT NEXT?

asking: "Why? Tell me more? What's so special about Him? How do I know Him so that I can love Him too?"

Let's answer that question: What is Christianity? What does it entail? Listen to what the Apostle Paul says about knowing Christ...

> But what things were gain to me, those I counted loss for Christ. Yea doubtless, and I count all things but loss for the excellency of the knowledge of Christ Jesus my Lord: for whom I have suffered the loss of all things, and do count them but dung, that I may win Christ, And be found in him, not having mine own righteousness, which is of the law, but that which is through the faith of Christ, the righteousness which is of God by faith: That I may know him, and the power of his resurrection, and the fellowship of his sufferings, being made conformable unto his death; If by any means I might attain unto the resurrection of the dead (Philippians 3:7-11).

The real heart of this chapter's study comes from the final part of that quote, but it's important to see the context leading up to those words. Paul is talking about all that he has achieved and all that he's lost since obeying the

Gospel. His point is to say it doesn't matter that he's lost a lot since coming to know Christ, because none of it compares to what he has in Christ.

Furthermore, all that he's achieved is worthless too, because none of it compares to what he has in Christ. That's why he says all that he's gained is "counted loss" for Christ. The phrase means he was willing to throw it all away if necessary to keep Christ in his life. Right after that, he says he has suffered the loss of all things, but that's okay with him because he's won Christ. Everything else in comparison is "dung."

That leads to the key portion of the text, wherein Paul gives his answer to the question "what is Christianity?" This is Paul's explanation for what it means to be a child of God and how it is a better life than whatever the world might offer.

What is Christianity? It is knowing Christ, and the power of His rising. It is sharing in His sufferings and conforming to His death. It is attaining resurrection of the dead and living with Him forevermore.

Do you see how Paul's summary begins and ends with a resurrection? It begins with me knowing **His** resurrection, and it ends with me attaining my **own** resurrection. Also, do you see also how Paul's words, and the order of things he

WHAT NEXT?

discusses, don't make any sense when considered from the standpoint of Jesus' life. The three things he mentions are out of order if he's talking about Jesus: They aren't listed forward or backward. If they were forward, it would be "sufferings, death, resurrection." If they were backward, it would be "resurrection, death, sufferings."

Instead, he mentions resurrection, then sufferings, then death. That doesn't make sense to think of it as a biography of Jesus, but it **does** make sense to think of it as a biography of the Christian life, and that even makes sense in the context too: Remember, Paul is talking about himself in this text. He's talking about all that he's won and lost and how none of it matters because Christ is all that matters.

So if nothing in your life matters except for Christ, then what is your life? What **is** Christianity? It is me knowing what the power of His resurrection means. It is me knowing what the fellowship of His suffering means. It is me knowing what conforming to His death means.

When you became a Christian, you put your worldly self to death, including all the loves and interests that consumed your mind and time. In their place, you took up Christ as your all in all. You had to put yourself to death to **become** a Christian, which means the first thing that happens **as** a Christian is a resurrection. You rise from the watery grave with a new life.

Naturally, as you start your new life, you will live in opposition to your old one. You don't do those things anymore. You don't talk like that anymore. You don't go to those places anymore. And the more you fill up your life with "not anymore," the more the world who "still does" those things grows annoyed, then frustrated, then angry, then—possibly—violent. The world pushes back and you suffer.

But that's okay because Jesus suffered too. So you and He have a kindred bond in suffering. You enjoy a "fellowship of suffering," if you will. Knowing that, you'll be okay with suffering. That doesn't mean it won't hurt; it will, but you'll endure it because you'll be armed with the knowledge that Jesus' suffering led to eternal glory, and yours will too. In between suffering and victory, however, is death. But, if He died for me, then I will take up my cross and conform to His death, sacrificing myself for Him.

What is Christianity? It's a life that began with a resurrection. Jesus said you must be born again (John 3:1-5) and since you have already been born the first time, all you had to do was figure out a way to do it again. Before that happened, though, you were alive in the world.

WHAT NEXT?

You lived and with your life you sinned and wasted the gift of life that God gave you. As a result, God's sense of justice was stirred, and He felt the compulsion to carry out vengeance against the one who sinned against Him.

Thankfully, God's sense of mercy was also stirred, and instead of vengeance, He offered Grace. How? By putting His vengeance onto His Son Jesus. Through the death of Christ, the penalty for your sins has been paid, opening the door to you putting your old sinful life to death, and rising with Jesus to a new life in God. You know Christ, in other words, and the power of His rising.

What is Christianity? It is a life that began with a resurrection...and led to suffering. Paul's words to Timothy are relevant here:

> *Persecutions, afflictions, which came unto me at Antioch, at Iconium, at Lystra; what persecutions I endured: but out of them all the Lord delivered me. Yea, and all that will live godly in Christ Jesus shall suffer persecution. But evil men and seducers shall wax worse and worse, deceiving, and being deceived (2 Timothy 3:11-13).*

MATTHEW L. MARTIN

You will suffer as a child of God. Peter said the same (1 Peter 4:16). Paul said as long as the world has evil people then those who do good will suffer. You will feel the heat; you will feel the pressure; you will wonder "is it worth it" to remain faithful to Jesus. And when you think you've finally overcome all the devil can throw at you, don't be surprised to discover the devil has even more he can throw at you.

Remember, however, that Jesus also suffered. Peter writes these words:

> *For this is thankworthy, if a man for conscience toward God endure grief, suffering wrongfully. For what glory is it, if, when ye be buffeted for your faults, ye shall take it patiently? but if, when ye do well, and suffer for it, ye take it patiently, this is acceptable with God. For even hereunto were ye called: because Christ also suffered for us, leaving us an example, that ye should follow his steps (1 Peter 2:19-21).*

If you do something wicked and are punished for it, there's nothing in that to rejoice. But, if you do good and suffer, then you have every reason to celebrate. Why? Because that means you're following in the footsteps of Jesus.

WHAT NEXT?

He suffered first; He left us an example. Remember, the Lord's invitation was not "take up an easy life and follow Me." He said "take up your cross and follow Me." Jesus did not promise us an easy life. He said His schooling was easy compared to the world (Matthew 11:28-30), but the world will continue to be hard and painful. Jesus never said it would be easy; He says it is worth it. You'll suffer, but He suffered too; share in the fellowship of suffering with Him.

What is Christianity? It is a life that begins with a resurrection. It is a life that leads to suffering. It is a life that ends in death...but not really. Nevertheless, you should consider death a distinct possibility. The moment may arise when you will have to choose between living with Jesus or dying for Jesus and, should that day come, I hope you will choose the latter and receive the crown of life promised to you (Revelation 2:10).

The fact is, no matter what happens, one of three things are certain to occur: Either you're going to live until Jesus returns, in which case it behooves you to be faithful, or you're going to live a long time and die of old age, in which case it behooves you to be faithful, or you're going to die in a sudden, unexpected, or possibly even violent way, whether that's as a direct result of your faith in Christ or via some freak accident.

MATTHEW L. MARTIN

However, it happens, if you're going to die, it behooves you to die faithful.

Paul, the man who wrote the text we're studying in this chapter, had his head chopped off. And yet, it is said that he was singing hymns as they led him to the chopping block. He woke up that morning knowing his life was going to end before the sunset, and he had enough faith and assurance in God to rejoice as they carried out his execution. How? What allowed him to have such conviction?

To know Christ is to love Him.

What is Christianity? It is a life that begins with a resurrection. It is a life that leads to suffering. It is a life that ends in death...but not really, because even if they kill you, through Christ you will rise again. You will receive a "crown" (2 Timothy 4:8).

In that case, you might be tempted to say Christianity begins with a resurrection and ends with eternal life, but even **that** wouldn't be entirely accurate because Christianity never ends. The life you have in Christ will never stop as long as you are faithful. There will come a moment, faster than the twinkling of an eye, when the trumpet sounds and the dead are raised to live forever (1 Corinthians 15:52).

WHAT NEXT?

As a preacher-mentor of mine, David Riley, once said: You don't "spend eternity" in Heaven because you can't "spend" eternity. It's not currency. You don't run out of it. It just keeps going. It is forever.

What is Christianity? It's the life you have with Jesus, world without end, Amen.

Chapter Fifteen

QUICK THOUGHTS TO CARRY WITH YOU...

There was never going to be a way to break down every possible question and concern a new Christian might have. I tried to think of the questions I had when I first put on Christ in baptism, but I understand that my experience is unique to me, just as yours is to you. Hopefully, the fourteen questions addressed in this book serve as a good foundation for you to build a faithful Christian life.

What else is there to say? A lot, I'm afraid. But if there has to be a "final" chapter to this study, I think it appropriate to dedicate it, not to any one particular idea, but to a quick, bullet

WHAT NEXT?

point list of thoughts that are important to remember as you begin your Christian walk. I'm inspired by the way Paul's first letter to Thessalonica ended with the Apostle offering short words of advice, encouragement, and commandment (1 Thessalonians 5:16-22).

To that end, here are some quick thoughts to carry with you...

1. NOTHING CAN SEPARATE YOU FROM THE LOVE OF CHRIST

I wouldn't recommend testing that theory, but then again it's not a theory; it's a fact. Paul specifically says nothing can separate you from the love of Christ (Romans 8:35-39).

Does that mean once you're saved you're always saved? No it does not. Jesus makes it clear that a forgiven person who doesn't forgive will lose his forgiveness (Matthew 18:21-35). You, a saved person, can go away from Christ, and discard the salvation He has given you. The good news is that a person who rejects Christ can always go back to Him to be forgiven again. Why? Because the love of Christ does not go away.

There is no height or depth or any other distance, factor, power, or force in existence that can stop God from loving you. Is there anything that can stop God from saving you? To that I would answer: You. Through Jesus, God gave you the power to become a child of His (John 1:12). That power is yours, provided to you by God's eternal love. You have the free will either to accept it, reject it, abandon it, or hold to it through thick and thin.

2. LOVE GOD
MORE THAN ANYTHING ELSE

When asked what is the greatest commandment in the Law of Moses, Jesus did not hesitate to give an answer. He could have said "oh, they're all good" but He didn't; He went straight for "love God with everything you've got" (Matthew 22:37).

Why not equivocate or comment on the sacredness of the **whole** Law? It's because Jesus understood that a person who loves God more than anything else is a person who will have no problem obeying any other command God gives.

When God is first, nothing else matters. When God is first, you'll do anything for Him. When God is first, you'll reject anything He opposes. Loving God is the secret to...everything. It's the thing that seems so obvious, but it's the

WHAT NEXT?

one thing most of God's people have the biggest trouble doing. That's not to say brethren don't love God. Many of them do; certainly they think they do.

The trouble is many do not love God more than everything else. Until that happens, you will find yourself constantly wrestling with your conscience. When God is not first, everything else becomes a new thing that might possibly be first, and that is an exhausting, indecisive life to live. Just make God the only thing you care to please and life will be so much easier.

3. LOVE EVERYONE ELSE
EVEN WHEN THEY DON'T LOVE YOU

Remember a whole page ago, when I said "when God is first, nothing else matters"? Yeah, about that: When asked what is the greatest commandment, Jesus didn't **just** say "love God with everything you've got." Even though the person asking the question was clearly only looking for a single answer, Jesus gave him two: "The second-greatest is like it; love your neighbor as you love yourself" (Matthew 22:39).

One of the ways I show my love for God is by loving others. When I help someone in need, that person might think "wow, that

Christian really loves me" but God sees me helping and says "my Christian really loves **Me**." If I only ever praise God, sing hymns to God, and talk about how great God is, and never do anything for anyone else, I am a liar, because how can I love God whom I have not seen, and not love others whom I can see (1 John 4:20)?

The trouble comes when other people aren't loving to you. It's easy to love God; look at all He's done for you. But the person who spits in your eye and laughs at your troubles is not so easy to love. It helps, then, to think of love, not as "an emotion reflecting warm feelings," but as "an action of service on behalf of another."

When we are good to people who are bad to us, we reflect the character of God, who sends the sunshine and rain on the deserving and the undeserving (Matthew 5:43-48). When we love those who hate us, we reflect the character of Christ who died for people who hated Him, us included (Romans 5:6-8).

It isn't easy to love hateful people, and it doesn't always result in an immediate reward. Sometimes, bizarrely, doing good to someone who is evil leads to them doubling down and doing more evil to you. Nevertheless, that's the life we live. That's the calling we answered. We were born again to be like Jesus; that means loving as he loved, not because it's easy but because it is godly.

WHAT NEXT?

4. You should probably be praying more

I don't want to be presumptuous. Maybe you're already praying quite a bit. It's just that I've observed over the years, both from personal experience and in talking with others, that when hardships arise, praying about it is not always the first thing that Christians think to do. When blessings come to us, praying with thanksgiving is not always the first thing brethren think to do. When small, petty problems pester and annoy us, we don't always think "I should pray about this."

And, if that's the case with you, then you should probably be praying more. However much you are praying each day, I'll bet you can squeeze in a few more minutes. Am I wrong? How easy is it to "vent" (complain) to a friend or colleague about something annoying? There's five minutes you could instead redirect to the throne of God in a constructive way.

How often have you sat on your bed, frustrated because you can't find your favorite pair of socks? Did you think to pray about it? You might think it's too small a thing to "bother" God with, but God is not a therapist who charges by the hour. Call Him. The number is toll-free and He's always ready to listen. You may think the problem is too small, but He understands that small problems add up. Nobody has just **one** small problem. Carrying one small rock in a sack is no big deal, but carrying a hundred of them is a weight too heavy to lug.

Give God your petty things (1 Peter 5:7).

As of this writing, I've got this black tie with a little red razorback embroidered on the bottom. I love that tie. I can't find it anywhere. Is it a minor thing? Yes. Does it affect anyone's salvation? No. Did I still ask God to help me find it? I sure did, and I didn't feel bad about it, either. God's not overworked. He doesn't have a lot on His plate. He has no plate. He's infinite!

Who in a Kingdom has the right to awaken the King in the middle of the night to ask for a glass of water? Not just anyone can knock on the door of their sovereign's chambers and make such a minor request. Who can? A little child of the King, that's who.

You're a Christian. You're a child of God. He sent Jesus to die for you so that you could have a relationship that was close enough and familial enough for you to bring any and every burden to Him.

Ask Him to help you find your socks!

WHAT NEXT?

5. LISTEN TO OLDER CHRISTIANS

They've been around longer than you. They've dealt with a lot of the same trials. They've asked a lot of the same questions. They've made a lot of the same mistakes.

In an era where people are abandoning religion in record numbers, finding someone who has been a faithful Christian for thirty, forty, fifty years is like striking gold. Those brethren have read their Bibles here and there, both for simple study and to help with a calamity, for so long they can recite verses from memory as effortlessly as you can quote your favorite movie.

Older Christians have seen the way the Devil operates. They've witnessed first-hand the horrors of sin and the rewards of faithfulness. While there is no substitute for the inspired Word, there is also no understating the value in having a conversation with someone who lives in the same world you do, who has the wisdom and perspective to see the sometimes obvious solutions you're missing. At the very least, there's no downside to the gentle encouragement they can bring.

MATTHEW L. MARTIN

6. REMEMBER CHRIST IS PERFECT; CHRISTIANS ARE NOT

Brethren will let you down. Yes, we should talk to older members, but they're not Jesus. They will make mistakes. Yes, we should lean on our peers, but they're not sinless. They have their own struggles and temptations. We should never stake our spiritual claim on how "like Christ" our brethren are (or aren't) because eventually they will let us down, and we will let someone down, too.

One of the most common attacks against Christianity relates to the perceived hypocrisy of Christians. First of all, it's not hypocritical to tell someone to stop sinning, even when you sometimes struggle with sinning, too. What **would** be hypocritical would be telling someone to stop when you aren't even trying to stop.

Second, even **if** a Christian is acting hypocritically, that's not a condemnation of Jesus or His church; that's a condemnation of that Christian. I refuse to let a so-called bad apple in the brotherhood tear down the whole church around him, and I will not put the hope of my salvation on the shoulders of someone who needs Jesus' blood just as much as I do.

WHAT NEXT?

7. YOU ARE GOING TO MESS UP

It doesn't have to be the end of the world when you sin, but that doesn't mean that it won't be. Whether or not it is depends on you. When you mess up, what are you going to do about it? Are you going to be arrogant and deny you did anything wrong? Are you going to be deflective and try to cast blame on others? Are you going to try and twist the scripture to justify your action, not only to soothe your guilty conscience but also to give yourself permission to continue in the sinful practice?

Or are you going to do what a Christian should do and repent? It frustrates me to hear the way some Christians talk about so-called "little sins." They say things like: "you really think one little sin will keep me out of Heaven?" Yes, I really do. I really think that.

One sin will keep you out of Heaven.

The issue is not the size of the sin. The issue is the stubbornness of the person who refuses to repent of it. It doesn't have to be a little sin; it can be the biggest, most heinous sin imaginable. Stop thinking of what you can get away with and still sneak in through the back door of Heaven, and start appreciating the awesomeness of God's grace. He can and will forgive the biggest sins, therefore all sins—big and small—are able to be forgiven, if they're repented of. If they're not, the soul that sins will die (Ezekiel 18:20), regardless of whether it's a "big" sin or a "small" one.

You're going to make mistakes. You're going to mess up. As a new Christian, you're going to assume things are okay that aren't, and you might even think some things are bad that are actually fine. You're going to slip into old habits from your old life.

What the Devil wants is for you to give up. He wants you to think it's impossible to be faithful. He wants you to feel the weight on your shoulders as you see other brethren around you seemingly having no problem being faithful. He doesn't want you to realize that all those other brethren have their own temptations and struggles that simply aren't being broadcasted for all to see.

Most of all, what the Devil wants is for you to fail to appreciate how readily available the saving power of Christ is. If we walk in the light as He is in the light, we have fellowship with God and the blood of Jesus, His Son, continually cleanses us of our sins (1 John 1:7). You're going to mess up, but if you stay in the light (through repentance and prayer), those sins are going to be cleansed along the way, every step you take toward Heaven.

WHAT NEXT?

8. You always have permission to serve.

There are brethren who have been Christians for twenty years that have never so much as led a prayer, or volunteered to cook a meal for someone who was grieving, etc. Why not? They would say: "no one has asked me."

I'm not going to say there aren't certain things you need permission/authority to do in the Lord's church; there are. What I **am** saying is you don't need to sit back and wait for someone to notice that you're ready to work. You **are** ready. The moment you came out of the water, you were ready to serve in the Kingdom.

If you just sit on the back row waiting for someone to come along and tell you it's okay to work, no one will ever come along because most will just assume you don't want to work. I know "announcements" are the worst part of a Sunday service, but listen carefully to what is said. Who is in need? What chores have to be done? What brother or sister that's involved in a project could use an extra pair of hands? Where can you help? What can you do?

Don't wait for permission to serve. God gave you permission by saving you and setting you in His Kingdom. Get to work!

MATTHEW L. MARTIN

9. THERE IS A ROLE FOR YOU, BUT...

Remember you're a servant, even if you're a leader. Someone once asked me how I defined a leader in the church. My answer is: A leader is a servant in the front of the line. The church of Jesus Christ has but one Leader, and that is our King, Jesus Christ. Everyone else submits to His sole authority.

There are those in His Kingdom who serve others, sight-unseen. They do the jobs no one notices. They help off-stage. They serve quietly in the background. There are also those roles that require someone front and center, someone pointing the way, someone directing traffic, scolding the wrong-doers, and encouraging the rest. God has given inspired qualifications for some specific leadership roles in His church, but regardless of whether or not you meet those qualifications, know this: There is **something** for you to do in the Kingdom.

And there is **nothing** for you to do, if you're going to do it with a "look at me" attitude. The Lord's church does not need spotlight-hogs. There is no place for pride in the Kingdom of Jesus. We are not called to seek the praise of men, or to do our work loudly, but to be quiet, meek, and humble, as even our Master was (Isaiah 53:7, Matthew 11:29, Philippians 2:8).

1O. Just be faithful

Those three words are forever etched into my brain thanks to a fellow MSOP student and friend, Stephen Sutton. "Just be faithful." You're not going to be perfect; just be faithful.

There's a hymn by Thomas Chisholm...

> *Oh! to be like Thee, blessed Redeemer,*
> *This is my constant longing and prayer;*
> *Gladly I'll forfeit all of earth's treasures,*
> *Jesus, Thy perfect likeness to wear.*

On the one hand, what a beautiful summary of the Christian ideology: What we seek is to be like Jesus; all our lives are devoted to the pursuit of His life. But look at those lyrics and tell me it's a "simple" undertaking. The singer tells God that he would gladly pay any price in order to wear the "perfect likeness" of Jesus. Oh, is that all? Just to be exactly like Jesus, that's your goal?

It reminds me of the time Philip said to Jesus: "Show us the Father and that will be sufficient" (John 14:8). Oh, is that all you require, Philip, just to see the Unseeable? Oh sure, that's not asking a lot!

It's a monumentally daunting undertaking to wake up in the morning and say to yourself "today, I'm going to be exactly like Jesus." I don't know about you, but I would probably fail before my feet even hit the floor!

And yet, the song has it right: That **is** the undertaking. That **is** the life. Will we ever achieve "perfect likeness"? I think not. But what a life we could live if we just tried!

Having said that, I spent four years in Higden, Arkansas serving under the legendary Gospel Preacher Carroll Sites. Carroll used to say that people love to talk about "doing their best" but, in his experience, few ever really did their best, at least not all the time.

Most of the time, people would "try" their best, but even that wasn't guaranteed. Trying your best all the time is exhausting. It's a high standard we rarely can maintain 24/7. Carroll liked to say that he started his day telling himself that he would "try to try" to do his best.

That's a pretty good life lesson from the former Drill Seargent turned soldier of Christ: Do your best. And when that fails, try again. And when you slip up, try to try to do better. Along the way, you might find yourself acting more and more like Jesus every day.

You're not going to be perfect. If you were, you'd have no need for Jesus. Instead, just be faithful. Just be faithful.

Just be faithful.

11. ACT LIKE A CHILD

I should probably clarify that the **kind** of child you should act like is the one Jesus calls to the Kingdom (Matthew 19:14). A proper child of God wants to be like his Father, wants to talk like Him, and go where He goes.

On the other hand, has there ever been a child who did not, at least once, hear a command from their parent, and ask "why do I have to?" Has there ever been a parent who has not employed, as the answer, the greatest come-back to that question that has ever been invented: "Because I said so."

In my experience, the response—while effective—also serves to frustrate the child in question. And when that child becomes a teenager, it's almost asking for a rebellion in response. I don't think the statement is a bad one, however. I just think we as parents can do a better job laying the foundation for **why** it is a good answer to the question.

There is no greater guidebook on parenting than the Bible, in particular the Old Testament. The relationship between God and Israel is, in a myriad of ways, akin to that of a father and his children. Through God's dealing with His nation, we see the Lord's patience, benevolence, compassion, sadness, and certainly His anger and retribution all on full display.

As you read the Old Testament, take note of the times when God gave a command to Israel that had clear and obvious (immediate) benefits to the ones obeying that command...

There was the command not to gather more manna than was needed for that day's meal: The consequence for disobeying would be bread that grew worms and became inedible. There was an obvious, immediate, consequence that the people could understand. It gave them an **additional** reason to obey.

There was the command not to ally themselves with pagan nations around them: The consequence for disobeying would be those godless nations turning on them and invading them, bringing misery and death to the people. There was an obvious, immediate, consequence that the people could understand. It gave them an **additional** reason to obey.

On the other hand, consider a command that had no immediate consequence: The Israelites were forbidden from eating pork. But what if a Jew bought a spiral ham from a pagan merchant and enjoyed a little feast on a random December? Would he get worms in his belly? No. Would some foreign army march through the streets chopping off heads? No. Would he sprout

WHAT NEXT?

a spiral tail from his backside like Dudley Dursley? No again. So what would happen in the immediate sense? How would breaking that command physically affect that person? It wouldn't. As a result, the natural question a person may ask is: So why give the command?

That question, however, is asked out of a selfish heart. It's asked by a person who only cares about how they are affected by disobedience. The proper heart—one that is in love with God—wouldn't worry about self; it would care only about pleasing God. In other words, sometimes God gives a command for no other reason than for His good pleasure. There may be secondary or tertiary reasons in the mind of God, but we're not privy to them. All we know is we are commanded to do certain things "because He said so."

And parents do that too.

Why do you sometimes randomly ask your kids to fetch something for you? Am I the only one who makes his child run from one end of the house to another to bring me a glass of water? Was I the only child who had one of those big honking cabinet TVs that didn't have a remote so I was the remote being summoned from my room right when I was in the middle of the

MATTHEW L. MARTIN

Tubular Level in Super Mario World just because the channel 7 news was on commercial and my dad wanted to see what was on the channel 4 news even though it's the same news dad just different people reciting the same four things that ever happened in Arkansas that day!

Sorry, where was I?

Am I the only one who gives their child a command that has no benefit to them but is solely for my own good pleasure? I doubt I am. And when my children ask me why they should, the answer is "because I asked you to." When a teenager wants to say being punished for disobeying is "unfair" because the command was "meaningless," the answer should be "it is not meaningless at all; it is what I want: That's the meaning."

Our children are being taught by their culture to believe there is no hierarchy to a home. They're being taught by culture to believe parents and children are equal and that if a parent wants to "request" something of a child, he must have a good reason, or he should expect that request to be challenged. They're being taught by culture to be selfish, to do only what serves their best interests, and to resist anything else.

WHAT NEXT?

What has been lost is the respect of inherent parental authority, and a lot of that is the fault of parents for not teaching our children Divine Principles: God is the ultimate parent, and He rightly gives commands sometimes that are solely given because it makes Him happy. He rightly punishes us for disobeying those commands, making it so that the punishment of God is the "only" negative consequence to breaking those commands.

And that should be enough.

It should be enough to be told "if you don't do it God will punish you." There should be no saying: "But that's not fair! Why should I have to do this just so that I don't get punished!" There should be none of that because there shouldn't be such a focus on self. The focus should be on pleasing God. If it is, then I won't see my life as a series of things I do to avoid being punished. What a miserable, cynical way to live that would be! Instead, I should see my life as a series of things I do to be well-pleasing to God.

And when that's the way you live your life, what a happy life you will have. When it's not— when your focus is on your own selfish wants and needs—then the reality of God's wrath toward the disobedient becomes a source of frustration, angst, and bitterness. It creates a tug of war between sovereign God and selfish man when there need not be a struggle at all. Let go of the rope; stop trying to drag God over to your side of the line. Humble yourself before God. Submit yourself below God. Draw yourself near to God and, when you do, God will draw near to you (James 4:6-8).

When that happens, you'll never even care about asking "why do I have to" obey His commands. Instead, you'll do what God commands because making Him happy will be what makes **you** happy. And what a happy (content, peaceful) life you'll have as a result.

Keep in mind, the same "unfair" God who is prepared to punish you for disobeying a seemingly arbitrary command, is the same "unfair" God who sent His Son to die for you so that you could be saved from the punishment He is prepared to give you!

God has two hands: One of forgiveness and one of punishment. Which one you take is up to you, but the only reason you even get a choice is because He gave you one. You want to talk about an unfair God? What's **fair** is a sinner being punished. What's **unfair** is a sinner being saved. You don't deserve to be saved. Be thankful you even have the option.

Because He said so.

WHAT NEXT?

CONCLUSION

This book was a collaborative process. The very idea for it came as a result of hearing a marvelous sermon (entitled "What Next?") from my long-time friend and football coach Caleb Shock. Many of the chapters came from my own personal experience learning my way around Christianity and the advice I was given by men wiser than I.

So many little nuggets of advice and wisdom have been picked up over the years and have etched themselves into my brain. I have written them here, but they came from someone else, who likely heard them from someone else

WHAT NEXT?

when **they** were just beginning **their** Christian walk. That's the beauty of God's Kingdom: We're all marching to Zion, helping each other along the way, one step at a time.

During the writing of this book, I reached out to a variety of preachers and elders, asking each of them a simple question: "Imagine you have just baptized someone, and they look at you and the first thing they say to you is: 'I'm saved now...what next?' What would your quick and simple statement of encouragement or motivation to them, to help them at the start of their Christian journey?"

Here's what they said...

MATTHEW L. MARTIN

"Always remember to keep your eyes focused on Jesus. Never turn back."

~ Jason Almond,
preacher @ Oppelo Church of Christ;
Oppelo, AR

WHAT NEXT?

"Take every opportunity to meditate on God's word, pray about everything in your life, and make choices that get you closer to Jesus!"

~ Dan Owen,
Instructor @ Bear Valley Bible Institute;
Denver, CO (by way of Paducah, KY)

MATTHEW L. MARTIN

"The test is not to do it all or to have all the answers. The test is to trust God. That is the test that I want to pass and I know you do as well. I promise you it will be worth it."

~ Stephen Sutton
preacher @ West Dyersburg Church of Christ; Dyersburg, TN

WHAT NEXT?

"You're newborn in Christ. So, just like a real baby, you need to focus on the basics, learning to walk and talk and eat basic Foods. Then work on emulating the adults around you, till you grow to maturity. But don't forget: Faith comes only from hearing the Word of God. So if you want to grow in your Christian faith, you are going to have to become a student of God's word, just watch other people."

~ George Hulett,
preacher @ Downtown Church of Christ;
Morrilton, AR

MATTHEW L. MARTIN

"This changes everything."

~ Danny Bohannan,
elder @ Higden Church of Christ;
Greers Ferry, AR

WHAT NEXT?

"Connect. Connect with God through the Bible and prayer. Connect with fellow Christians by spending time with them. Connect with the lost by doing good wherever you see the opportunity and giving a reason for the hope that's now in you."

~ Kevin Feeler,
elder @ Higden Church of Christ;
Greers Ferry, AR

MATTHEW L. MARTIN

"We will do this together. Christians help Christians. Let's work together!"

~ David Riley,
preacher @ Mars Hill Church of Christ,
consummate local evangelist;
Vilonia, AR

WHAT NEXT?

"Salvation is not a one-time something that we obtain, but a way of life that we continue."

~ Ted Knight,
Traveling evangelist,
Sage of the Natural State;
Conway, AR

MATTHEW L. MARTIN

"Share your excitement with someone you know or someone you meet. When they ask why you are so excited about what God has done for you, simply say: "Come and see." Invite them to come and see how God can change their lives as He has yours."

~ Bob Turner,
Director of S.A.L.T. (Sunset Academy of Leadership Training) for Sunset International Bible Institute, a true mentor;
Virginia Beach, VA

WHAT NEXT?

"Always do the Lord's work. Never be selfish. Put Him first. You're married to Christ. Act like it. Be faithful to your Spouse."

~ Jesse Ellison
Personal evangelist the likes of which
the state of Arkansas has never seen;
Wooster, AR

MATTHEW L. MARTIN

"Fall deeper in love with Jesus every day and make sure that everything you do is something that will bring glory to God."

~ Dan Winkler,
Bible Scholar, Teacher, Student, Preacher,
our brotherhood's finest living scholar;
West Tennessee and around the globe

WHAT NEXT?

"Relax and enjoy. **Relax** because you are no longer in sin and under condemnation. You can breathe again. **Enjoy** because you have received a free gift (forgiveness of sins) that would be impossible without Jesus' death on the cross. Take a moment just to relax and enjoy your salvation."

~ Barry Grider,
preacher @ Riverbend Church of Christ,
greatest pulpiteer I've ever known;
Dalton, GA

MATTHEW L. MARTIN

"You are not alone. You are my sibling in
Christ now. If you have any questions,
or if you make any mistakes, you call me.
I've had them or made them, too. Call
me or I'll call you."

~ Allan Myers
Elder @ Robinson & Center Church of Christ,
Genuine counsellor, mentor, friend;
Conway, AR

WHAT NEXT?

"Next? Next you live.
You get a fresh start.
Use it to His glory."

~ Me,
Batesville, AR

MATTHEW L. MARTIN

"Now the work begins."

~ Chris Eubanks,
The man who baptized me;
Searcy, AR

WHAT NEXT?

ABOUT THE AUTHOR

Matthew Martin is a thirty-something
husband and father of three.

He is a 2002 graduate of
Wonderview High School,
and a 2005 graduate of
Memphis School of Preaching,
from which he received a
Bachelor's Degree in Biblical Studies.
He also has a Master's Degree
in Biblical Studies from
Bear Valley Bible Institute.

He spent three years as a Youth and Associate
Minister with the Forest Hill church of Christ
in Germantown, TN, as well as four years
preaching for the Higden Church of Christ in
Greer's Ferry, AR, and seven years preaching
for the church of Christ in Guy, AR.

He currently preaches for the North Heights
Church of Christ in Batesville, AR.

MATTHEW L. MARTIN

OTHER BOOKS FROM THE AUTHOR

Verse-by-Verse commentaries on every book of the New Testament are available, as well as several from the Old Testament.

A full catalogue is available at:
booksbymatthew.com/bookstore-spiritual

Study books include...

WHAT NEXT?

DESPISED

YOU ARE NOT **DESPISED** BY GOD

**ADVICE FOR
YOUNG PEOPLE
STANDING
ON THE BRINK**

BY
MATTHEW
L. MARTIN

LET
NO MAN
DESPISE
YOUR
YOUTH...
(1 TIMOTHY 4:12)

MATTHEW L. MARTIN

FROM PARADISE TO PARADISE

WHAT NEXT?

COMING SOON

Parental Advice from the
HEAVENLY FATHER

Matthew
L. Martin

MATTHEW L. MARTIN

COMING SOON

WHAT NEXT?

MANY THANKS

This book only exists because Caleb Shock blew me away with his Friday Night sermon at Camp Areopagus in 2021.

His lesson, simply entitled "What Next?" explored the basic idea at the heart of this book: What do you say to someone who is just beginning their Christian walk?

Caleb's sermon inspired me, and I thank him for it, and for the many years of friendship he and I have shared. This book goes to him.

Thanks also are owed to the other three speakers—friends and mentors all—who spoke that week at camp: Jason Almond, Chris Eubanks, and David Riley.

Special thanks as well go to Allan Myers, who remains a steadfast example of faithfulness, a tremendous role model, and a priceless encourager.

Above all, thanks be to God. "What next?" is the question we ask because we do not know what tomorrow holds. We **do** know who holds tomorrow, however, and what a blessing it is to know that He holds our hand. Whatever comes "next," we will step into it safe and secure in the Savior's gentle grasp.